The Natural Nine
Cooking with Whole Grains

The Natural Nine
Cooking with Whole Grains

Lorraine Dilworth Tyler

Magic Mill, Division of SSI, Salt Lake City, Utah

Library of Congress
Catalog Card Number
ISBN 0-9609832-1-X

Copyright © 1984, Magic Mill

Printed in the United States of America.

Contents

Foreword

Lorraine Tyler's interest in whole grains began when the first of her children was just a toddler. As a conscientious new mother, Lorraine asked a nutritionist she knew and respected which diet would be best for her new family.

The nutritionist advised her to use lots of whole grains in her family's diet, and little sugar.

At that time, Lorraine was not aware of any whole grain cookbooks being available at the time. A quick, but thorough, search at bookstores confirmed it. She was on her own.

Undaunted, Lorraine set out on her own to make something palatable out of what she termed as "that ugly brown flour." She reluctantly admits, after a little questioning, that her whole wheat bread was barely suitable for human consumption on the first day, and could be used effectively as a doorstop on the second!

Lorraine persevered, however, and quickly began to discover the best way to cook with whole grains. In no time at all, the aroma of freshly baked whole wheat bread filled her home . . . bread that was every bit as delicious and nutritious as it smelled.

This experience helped Lorranie compile a small cookbook that became the predecessor of her popular "The Magic of Wheat Cookery," which has introduced the joys of whole wheat cooking to nearly 300,000 readers.

Lorraine, a resident of beautiful Walnut Creek, California, brings a varied background to **The Natural Nine.** In addition to being a wife, mother of seven, and grandmother of eighteen, she is an accomplished musician and genealogist.

Lorraine loves to garden and crochet, and is learning to knit. She has been a Magic Mill distributor since 1973, and also holds a lifetime certificate for teaching whole grain cooking in the California Adult Education Program. In her "spare" time, Lorraine has given over three hundred dinners and/or lectures on the value of whole grains across the United States and in Canada.

In working with the many different varieties of whole grains, Lorraine has become aware of their great importance to our well-being. We hear of the virtues of rice for the Orient, the value of millet for the people of India and Africa, rye for the northern Europeans, oats for the Scotsman, and corn for the native Americans. Lorraine has helped us see that from country to country, continent to continent, whole grains have the capability of building strong bodies and clear minds.

Lorraine is eager for others to learn this important lesson, and to improve their family's health by using the recipes in **The Natural Nine.**

Magic Mill has enjoyed a long and valued association with Lorraine Tyler. We have enjoyed working with her from the days of the original, stone-grinding Magic Mill home flour mill (over ten years ago) to go the ultra-modern, industry-leading Magic Mill III Plus™ of today.

Lorraine's charm, down-home quality, and expertise in whole grains live in this cookbook and are embodied in its recipes. We take great pleasure in bringing you her second comprehensive whole grain cookbook, which is destined to be every bit as successful as her first—**The Natural Nine.**

MAGIC MILL

The Bosch 4-in-1 Kitchen Center

The Bosch 4-in-1 Kitchen Center is rated by cooking professionals the world over as the most complete and sophisticated kitchen machine available for home use today.

It is actually four machines in one: a mixer, blender, food processor and breadmaker. The Bosch 4-in-1 Kitchen Center slices, kneads, chops, blends, grates, mixes, and much, much more.

Famous German Bosch engineering results in long, low-maintenance performance. The Bosch 4-in-1 Kitchen Center is 550 watts strong and is UL or CSA approved.

It is powerful enough to knead heavy bread dough, yet gentle enough to whip the lightest souffle.

A machine this good deserves an equally good warranty. The Bosch 4-in-1 Kitchen Center is warranted for three full years from the date of purchase.

Magic Mill III Plus™ Flour Mill

The Magic Mill III Plus™ is the world's finest home flour mill. Through its patented micro-milling™ process, all grains—including corn and soybeans—are quickly refined into low-temperature, high-nutrient flour.

The Magic Mill III Plus™ unlocks the natural goodness, vital nutrition, and essential fiber in whole grains. It produces fresh flour for your everyday use.

This mill offers a 19-cup stainless steel flour pan, 6-cup grain hopper, easy texture selection, automatic internal cleaning, UL or CSA approval, and unrivaled milling performance!

Best of all, the Magic Mill III Plus™ comes with a two-year limited warranty—and LIFETIME limited warranty on the milling heads!

No other mill offers you all that. No other mill ever comes close.

Preface

"Bread appears on every page of history, deeply rooted in the legacy of all mankind. It comes in many shapes and sizes. Each with a heritage. Each with a tradition . . . light . . . dark . . . raised . . . flat . . . hard . . . soft . . . round . . . square . . . crusty . . . crackly . . . enriched . . . some with fruit . . . some with spices . . . with onions and with cheese.

"It's Swedish, English, Italian, Hungarian, French, Jewish, and Sour Dough. And as American as a hot dog. It makes toast and a sandwich. It carries peanut butter to the roof of your mouth and gets jam on your cheek. It's a texture, a taste and a smell of home. The only food you can eat three times a day, day in and day out, and never tire of it."

My fascination with this versatile, beautiful food led to a love for grains. As my interest grew in the characteristics and uses of these grains, I realized that many people, including myself, knew little of the value or use of grains in the diet. So with the aid of my Magic Mill and my Bosch Kitchen Machine, my kitchen became a proving ground and my family served as judges.

Together we discovered much about grain: Grains may be cooked individually or in combinations. We should have whole grains every day, along with other nutritious foods. Grain should be whole and unaltered by man. To get the maximum nutritional value from any grain, it should be ground just before using. Grains are satisfying, budget-reducing, and delicious.

A person can spend a lifetime learning all the facets of whole grains. I have been years compiling this book, and I realize that I have just a good start. Many of you probably have experience with whole grains and recipes that you enjoy. Try these recipes and make your own adaptations. The combinations of grains are never-ending and, therefore, ever interesting. Realizing that nearly all grains combine well, do not hesitate to try other grains besides the ones listed.

In developing recipes for this book, I have tried to select a wide variety. Some recipes contain sugar, some do not. Some recipes use meat, some do not. The important thing is that every recipe contains a whole grain. Often the grain is milled; sometimes it is undried, such as fresh or frozen corn. Sometimes a little all-purpose flour has been added for lightness, but every recipe contains a whole grain in its unaltered and pure form, with no deletions.

This book is written for use with any grain mill or kitchen appliance capable of mixing heavy dough.

However, my personal preference and experience has been with the compact Magic Mill III Plus™ and the wonderful Bosch Kitchen Machine. These two appliances have served me so well that I can heartily recommend them to anyone who does not presently own a flour mill or bread mixer. The recipes within this book refer to these appliances, but they may be adapted to other mills and mixers.

I want to express my gratitude to the many people who have encouraged and assisted me with this book. Thank you to my husband, Lynn, and my children and their families, Dawn and James Smith, Rebecca and David Tyler, and Klea and Bret Wolz, who have supported me through trial and triumph. From my hometown of Carey, Idaho, I have had the help of my brother, Arlen Dilworth, and Shirl Reay and Boyd Stocking. Edwin and Donna Hahn of Wallace, Nebraska, and Earl and Louise Hamilton of Glynn, Arkansas, have also been of assistance.

I also want to acknowledge the help of Linda Prusse for editing this cookbook and styling much of the food for photography. Also thanks to Jim McLaughlin, graphic design, and John Jelte and Bob Pennington, photographers. Their talents in book production created a truly professional product.

I have spent eight years compiling, testing, and preparing this cookbook. During these years I have worked with many fine people at Magic Mill, and they have been a constant inspiration to me. I have enjoyed many years as a distributor of the excellent Magic Mill products and appreciate the many people through this association who have been a help to me.

This cookbook is only a smattering of the multiplicity of uses for grains. I hope it will inspire your creativity. Remember as you prepare and share these whole grain dishes with your friends and neighbors that these dishes carry a message; they say that you welcome your neighbor's friendship. Take them to the sick and elderly and they say "I care." Share the preparation with a child and they say "I love you." Bake them for your family and they change a house into a home.

Magic Aire II™ Dehydrator

Nothing captures and preserves the fresh-picked flavor and nutrition of fruits, vegetables, and meats like the Magic Aire II™ dehydrator.

The Magic Aire II's™ 100% solid state controls keep the temperature in the drying chamber at a space-age constant. This reduces drying time and minimizes nutrient and flavor loss.

Ten stackable trays hold over ¼ bushel of produce. You save money by using only the exact number of drying trays needed: up to ten, or as few as two.

The Magic Aire II™ is UL or CSA approved, and comes with a two-year limited warranty.

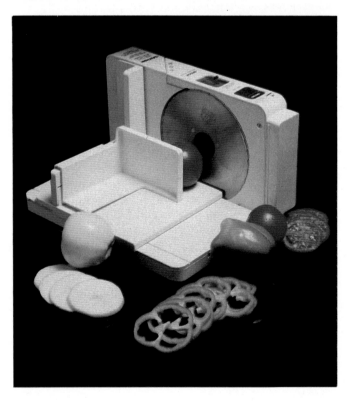

Bosch Electronic Slicer

Slicing food for dehydrating is made beautifully simple and amazingly fast with the Bosch Electronic Slicer.

Foods that are sliced to a uniform thickness dry faster and better. That's why the Bosch Electronic Slicer is the Magic Aire II's™ ideal dehydrating companion.

But it does more. Homemade bread is effortlessly and evenly sliced. Cheese and meat may be purchased in bulk (saving you money), sliced, wrapped and frozen for later use.

The Bosch Electronic Slicer is UL approved, and comes with a one-year limited warranty.

The Natural Nine

Barley

History

Barley, probably the first cereal grain cultivated by man, is an ancient food. Early traces of barley in Egypt date this cereal back to 3000-5000 B.C.

References to barley are found throughout the ancient histories of Egypt, Mesopotamia, Europe, and China. In the Old and New Testaments, barley is often associated with a land of plenty or a measure of payment. Anciently, barley and wheat were used as units of weight. Great festivals have coincided with the harvesting of this grain. Its praises are sung in mythology. Jesus fed five thousand followers on five barley loaves and two fish.

In the early seventeenth century, English colonists, Dutch immigrants, and Spanish settlers brought barley to America. Today, barley is the fifth-ranking grain in terms of consumption, surpassed only by wheat, rice, corn, and oats.

Description

Over 2,000 varieties of barley exist. The best known and most frequently planted kinds fall into the following categories:

Six-row barley grows with its spike notched on opposite sides. Three spikelets at each notch develop into a kernel. Thus, the head has a square appearance. The six-row barley has a short head—usually about two inches long.

Two-row barley has central florets that produce grain and lateral florets that are sterile. These heads can grow up to six inches long.

Irregular barley is the least cultivated. It has fertile central florets and varying proportions of fertile or sterile lateral florets.

Malting barley comes from both six-row and two-row barley. However, the six-row Manchurian barley seems to be used most frequently. The two-row Stepto and Perline are also common.

Production

Barley can tolerate the greatest climatic range and soil conditions of all the cereal grains. It is highly resistant to drought. It will grow in cool, mountainous areas as well as in the warmer climates; in subarctic as well as in subtropical climates.

Barley grows best in a cool, moist climate. It matures in a ninety-day period and requires a good soil to produce a good crop. However, the soil should have a low nitrogen content or the plants may droop. On an average, more pounds of barley can be produced per acre than oats or wheat.

Uses and Storage

Barley should have a moisture content of 13 percent or less. For maximum storage, store in an airtight container.

This grain cannot be used alone in a yeast bread. It has a low gluten content; thus, the gas simply escapes into the air and prevents the dough from rising. However, barley is very useful in making barley cakes, flatbreads, or muffins.

Commercially, barley is used as a breakfast food and is pearled for use in soups. Malting barley has much more food value than pearl barley. Pearl barley has been rolled until some of the outer aleurone layer has been removed. It takes 100 pounds of barley to produce 35 pounds of pearl barley. The aleurone layer is used to make stock feed or baby cereal.

The barley plant itself is sometimes used for stock feed. More than half the barley grown in the United States is fed to livestock.

Barley is an essential ingredient of a light, whole grain cake. When using whole wheat flour, or even all-purpose flour, substitute 2 tablespoons of barley flour for 2 tablespoons of wheat flour in each cup of flour used. It will add lightness to the cake.

Barley mixed with wheat flour may also be used to make cream puffs and pastries. Porridge and soup thickeners are also made with barley. Barley flour, arrowroot starch, or cornstarch may be interchanged.

Barley tea or broth is strength-giving and especially good in cold weather. Use barley that has as much of the aleurone layer remaining as possible.

Barley is a nongas-forming grain (alkaline) and is easy to digest. It contains about the same amount of carbohydrates as corn with more protein but slightly less fat.

Sprouting

Not all barley will sprout. In fact, most of what is prepared for human consumption will not sprout. A malting barley or seed barley must be purchased for this purpose. Malting barley is the foundation for beer or any liquor in which malt is used.

To make malt, the barley is steeped in warm water and allowed to sprout. This steeping produces the enzyme diastase, which changes the starch into sugar under the proper conditions. The malt, in turn, affects the raw grain used in the brewing process. After the barley has sprouted, it is dried in a kiln and ground into a powder that is used to flavor milkshakes and candies and to make malt syrup used in rolls and breads.

Home Grinding Procedures

Barley may be ground easily with most stone mills and with the Magic Mill III Plus™.

Buckwheat

History

Buckwheat is a native plant of central Asia. It is recorded in history as being a staple of Mongolia and the Georgian area of Russia. The Chinese used buckwheat for hundreds of years before it was carried to Europe by travelers and then brought to America by German and Dutch settlers.

Description

Buckwheat is three-sided in form, gray in color, and encased in a dark gray husk. It is not a member of the grass family as are other grains. Buckwheat belongs to the same family as sorrel. However, it has been included in this book as a grain because of its nutritive value. As the grass family grows with a long, slender leaf, the buckwheat plant has a heart-shaped leaf, grows to a height of about three feet, and blossoms into clusters of beautiful, fragrant white flowers. Each flower has the potential of developing a seed. Bees pollinate the seed, enabling it to produce. Thus, buckwheat becomes an important source of a particularly delicious, dark honey.

Buckwheat contains 73 percent starch, 2.2 percent fat, and 10 percent protein. It also contains thiamin, niacin, riboflavin, phosphorous, fat, calcium, iron, carbohydrates, B complex, vitamin E, and rutin. Buckwheat contains 1,510 calories per pound dry weight.

Production

Buckwheat grows best on well-drained soils in a cool climate. However, it will grow in marshy, hilly, and poor soil where no other grain will grow. It is sometimes used as a "green manure" to help increase the quality of poor producing soils. As a green manure crop, the buckwheat grows to the blossom stage and is then plowed under. Buckwheat grows quickly and can be used as a late season crop. It is hardy and resists insects and disease. Buckwheat plants can kill weeds in a field by shutting out the sunlight from the weeds or by smothering them in their growth. Probably due to its distinctive flavor, buckwheat is not grown extensively. People either enjoy its flavor or completely reject it.

Uses

Buckwheat is often grown to be used in feeding livestock. Sheep are pastured on its greens, and England uses the buckwheat groat to feed pheasants. For human consumption, it is an excellent cereal and has a wonderful flavor. In the United States, it is principally used as flour in pancakes. However, in central Asia and Russia, it is made into kasha, in which the whole groat is cooked as a cereal. Onions, meats, vegetables, and spices are often added, and it becomes similar to the rice or bulgur pilaf of Middle East fame.

Although buckwheat cannot be used alone in making yeast breads, it does make an excellent crepe. It may also be substituted, in part, in most whole kernel grain recipes. In some recipes, buckwheat is added for its distinctive flavor. It is excellent when combined with wheat flour in a 50-50 ratio or in a buckwheat and whole wheat ratio of 35-65.

Sprouting

Sprouting brings chlorophyll and vitamin C into the buckwheat. To sprout buckwheat, its husk must still be intact. It is best to grow buckwheat sprouts in a shallow pan of soil. The husks will remain in the soil and the cuttings of the tender, young plants may be used in salads or enjoyed as a snack food.

Buckwheat is rich in minerals and vitamins, especially vitamin E and B complex. Rutin, a key ingredient in buckwheat, is available in the seed or in the sprout. When sprouted, the amount of rutin is magnified many times.

Home Grinding Procedures

Buckwheat can be a difficult grain to grind with a stone mill. The Magic Mill III Plus™ efficiently grinds buckwheat with or without the husk.

Corn

History

In early history, the term **corn** was the name given to all grains and was used to indicate the principle cereal crop of a locality. Several different grains used in Biblical accounts are called corn. In England, corn means wheat. In Scotland, it means oats.

Corn, as we know it today, is a native cereal grain of the Americas. No evidence exists of its existence in the "civilized" or European world until Columbus discovered it in America. At that time, the native Americans were cultivating several different types of corn. Through trading, these early Americans developed and hybridized almost all of the strains of corn in use today.

Evidence of corn use is found among many artifacts of the leading Indian tribes of North and South America. The oldest evidence actually found in South America goes back to about 1000 B.C. Corn was even found in an excavation 200 feet below the present Mexico City.

Corn was grown by nomadic tribes as well as the highly civilized Mayas of Central America, the fierce Aztecs, and the Incas of Peru. Corn produced an abundant harvest and was easily grown so it allowed these ancient people time for weaving, making pottery and fine jewelry, and building magnificent highways and classic pyramids.

Columbus carried seeds of corn to the Old World, and in two generations it spread over Europe, Africa, India, China, and Tibet. A Chinese emperor even taxed it! The rapid spread of corn outdistanced the spread of tobacco. Nevertheless, in certain areas of the world, corn was and still is considered food only for animals.

When the Pilgrims arrived on the American continent, their chances for survival appeared bleak. Their stores of foodstuffs were running low, and starvation was imminent. The Indians took pity on them and shared their supplies of corn. The new settlers were taught by the Indians how to plant, cultivate, and enjoy this wonderful food. Without this aid, the Pilgrims' survival would have been questionable.

Corn is currently a major food source for both humans and animals in the Americas, particularly in Mexico and Central America. In the United States, it is the most valuable crop grown.

Description

Corn grows in climates ranging from the cold of northern Russia to the heat of South America. It grows at below sea level and at 12,000 foot heights in Peru. A crop of corn matures somewhere in the world every month of the year. In the United States, corn ranks second in production to wheat. In world production, it is surpassed by wheat and rice.

Corn is extremely high in magnesium. It also contains thiamin, niacin, riboflavin, fat, magnesium, calcium, sodium, protein, carbohydrates, potassium, iron, vitamin A, and phosphorus. Corn contains 1,651 calories per dry pound weight. The nutritional values of the different types of corn may vary.

Dent corn, also known as field corn, is grown principally for livestock feed. The stalk and corn are often made into silage. It is not a tasty corn for the table, although white dent corn is made into hominy. When it dries, a dent develops in the top of each kernel, hence its name.

Sweet corn has the best flavor of any type of corn as it contains twice as much sugar as dent corn. It is grown entirely for human consumption. The flavor of sweet corn is best the day it is picked. It can be steamed over water, boiled, baked in its husks in hot coals, or eaten raw. The finest nutrition that corn has to offer can be obtained by enjoying corn raw on the cob.

Flour corn is principally grown by the natives of America from the southwestern United States to South America. It is not grown commercially. In Peru, Bolivia, and Ecuador, a large seed variety has been developed, with seeds ranging up to one inch in length and nearly one inch wide. These soft kernels are easily ground by hand.

Flint corn, also known as "colorful corn," has colored kernels ranging from white to deep red. The kernel is very hard, hence the name. Flint corn is found in New England and Wisconsin, but it is principally grown in South America. It has a short growing season and transports easily. Argentina exports much of this type of corn. Ground into cornmeal, flint corn is particularly delicious.

Popcorn, with its hard, rather pointed kernel, is a favorite snack food. It is often the only whole grain available in today's supermarkets. Because it is a whole grain, its nutrients remain intact. It provides minerals, proteins, and vitamins, including vitamin E and B complex.

Cornmeal which has been commercially prepared has been degerminated; the germ, the corn oil, and the protein casing holding them in the center of the kernel have been removed. Corn is degerminated because when it is ground with its oil, it becomes rancid and does not store well. Thus, commercial cornmeal is a product with the life forces missing. It is better to grind popcorn, home dehydrated corn, or dent corn to receive all the food value corn offers at the most inexpensive price.

Corn flour is made by grinding cornmeal to a finer consistency. It is often used when a recipe calls for cornmeal.

Uses

Corn takes many forms—from the corn tortilla of Mexico to good old popcorn. Soups, breads, breakfast foods, corn flakes, hominy, corn oil, corn whiskey, tamales, grits, and corn flour are all made with this wholesome grain. Other products made from corn range from starches, dextrins, syrups, and dextrose to adhesives and chemicals. For much of the beer and whiskey market, corn is the foundation.

The entire stalk of corn has many industrial uses. The stalk can become silage, paper, and wallboard. The husk becomes filling material. Cobs are used to make fuel, charcoal, industrial solvents, and corn cob pipes.

Home Grinding Procedures

If using a stone mill, grind corn coarsely as it has a tendency to glaze the stones. It may also be mixed with wheat and ground into a fine flour.

In the Magic Mill III Plus™, grind corn on the coarse setting, producing a slightly coarse flour. Any type of dried corn may be used when grinding cornmeal.

MILLET

History

Millet, used by prehistoric man, is one of the oldest known grains. Pythagoras, the Greek philosopher and mathematician, urged the use of it in 500 B.C. It predated rice in China and was common fare in and around the Holy Land during Biblical times.

Millet continues to be a valuable food crop throughout the world. It is used from French West Africa to Korea and Japan. Russian peasants often eat it three times a day. The Hunzas of northern India extensively use millet and are purported to be the healthiest people in the world.

Description

Millet is a nonfattening grain, a complete food, and it provides a good balance of amino acids. It is high in minerals, especially calcium, and contains all the essential amino acids. It also has more vitamins than any other grain, offering the complete vitamin B complex including B 17. Millet is alkaline and is easily digested.

Millet contains the following nutrients: thiamin, calcium, riboflavin, carbohydrates, iron, lecithin, phosphorous, niacin, fat, potassium, and protein. Millet has 1,483 calories per pound dry weight.

One-third of the world's population depends on millet as its cereal grain. In the United States, however, it is used principally for bird seed or chicken feed. The plant itself is grown as pasture for hay or for livestock consumption.

Some types of millet are best when used with the hulls on. Egyptian and Indian pearl millet can be hulled quite easily, but hulling is more difficult with other types of millet. Perhaps for this reason it is often eaten with the hull on. The hull gives the millet a completely different flavor. Millet is a cream-colored seed and is harvested similar to wheat.

Production

Millet grows best in rich, loamy soils. However, it will also grow in low fertility soils and with little moisture. It grows to a height of 10 feet, depending on the type, and is an annual, warm season plant.

Uses

Millet is usually boiled, steamed as a cereal, or ground and used as flour. It is one of the most nutritious cereals in the world and is often used in vegetarian loaves, pilafs, grits, meal for pancakes, and flour for breads. When used as flour, the flavor may be a bit strong. Browning the flour improves its flavor when used alone in a recipe. It is usually mixed with whole wheat flour for baking. Chapati bread is made from a 50-50 mixture of these two flours.

Home Grinding Procedures

Hulled millet grinds easily in a stone grinder, but unhulled millet can be a challenge. Hand feed, and don't grind too much grain at a time as it tends to overheat the motor. Millet is easily ground in the Magic Mill III Plus™.

Oats

History

In 1772, Dr. Samuel Johnson made this statement to James Boswell, a Scot: "Oatmeal! Food for horses in England and men in Scotland."

Boswell made this historic reply: "Aye, and where will you find such horses or such men?"

Oats were first identified as a weed in barley in southwest Asia and were probably transported with barley as people migrated. Within time, oats were isolated from barley and were found to be palatable. They began to be grown for the first time as a food crop in central Europe. From Europe, they were brought to the British Isles. They were not identified as a food in early Christian history, but by the thirteenth century the British were growing oats, calling it "pilcorn." Oats thrive in a cool, moist climate and consequently grew exceptionally well in Scotland.

For many years, oats were used as a bartering agent or as part of a man's wage in Scotland. Prior to World War II, many men were paid a weekly wage of 1¼ to 1½ pounds of oats. Wages also included 1 ton of coal every 6 months, 1 load of firewood every 6 months, 1 ton of potatoes annually, 3 pints of milk daily, and 140 pounds of oatmeal every 6 months. Children who were attending school came home for their allotment of the father's wages in staples.

Description

Oats are used in five different forms:

Groat is the soft kernel of the oat. After the oat is husked, the remaining oat groat can be eaten in its raw, natural state. It is good when softened overnight and added to bread, to a pot of stew, or used as cereal.

Steel-cut oats are oat groats that have been cut into two or three pieces. They may be used in the same manner as whole oats. Steel-cut oat cereal will have a different texture than whole oat groat cereal.

Rolled oats are oat groats that have passed through a steam chamber and been partially cooked. They are then flattened between rollers, dried, and packaged. Each flake is one oat groat; notice the rib down the center of each flake.

Quick oats are processed in a manner similar to rolled oats. They are steel-cut, passed through a steam chamber, partially cooked, rolled, and packaged. Quick oats are flatter than rolled oats and will cook more quickly. If a recipe specifically calls for quick oats, use them. A substitution may affect the resulting product.

Oat flour is made from milling whole oats. It is a natural deterrent to spoilage. Bread made with certain types of oat flour will not spoil as fast as it would using other flours. Oat flour is excellent for cookies, as are rolled oats and quick oats.

The nutritive value of steel-cut oats, rolled oats, quick oats, and oat flour is virtually the same. The known nutrients are thiamin, niacin, riboflavin, fat, protein, chlorine, iodine, carbohydrates, iron, vitamin E, calcium, sulphur, fluorine, ash, and silicon. Oats contain 1,769 calories in one pound of dry weight.

Production

Oats are one of the most important cereal crops. They are grown in the cooler and more temperate regions of the world, although some hearty species grow near the Arctic circle. Oats can extract nutritional ingredients from soils that other grains, except rye and buckwheat, cannot. In fact, oats need a soil that is not extremely rich. When grown in nitrogen-rich soil, they droop.

The United States is the largest producer of oats, with Russia and Canada close behind. Scotland is also a major producer of this fine grain.

Uses

About 90 percent of all oats grown are fed to livestock. They are especially good for horses. Oat straw is used for feed and fertilizer.

The virtues of oats are myriad. The oat is the only grain that comes through the processing chamber with the same food value it goes in with. It remains virtually intact, including the germ. As a result, oats have many nutritional uses.

Oats offer a higher protein content than any other cereal grain. Oatmeal is a great strength-giver. Oatmeal water is a healthy, renewing drink. Rolled oats are particularly good as a porridge. Oat flour mixed with warm milk makes an excellent baby food.

Home Grinding Procedures

Home stone mills do not grind oats well because of the softness of the kernel. The pores of the stones get plugged with the flour, and the motor overheats. To help eliminate this problem, open the stones as far as they will go and feed the oats through slowly. The end result resembles oatmeal with flour mixed in. This combination is completely usable. The Magic Mill III Plus™ easily grinds oats into a very fine flour.

Rice

History

Rice has been growing for thousands of years in Southeast Asia. Traces of its history have been found in India dating back to 3000 B.C. Interestingly, rice is not mentioned in the Bible. It must not have been native to the Holy Land, or perhaps it did not have the prominence of some of the other grains. The Greeks learned of rice about 326 B.C. when Alexander the Great invaded India, found it growing there, and carried some seeds home to Greece. The Moors introduced rice to Spain about 700 A.D. The Spaniards then took it to Italy about 1400 A.D. and on to the West Indies and South America in the early 1600s.

Rice was first introduced to North America in 1686 when a ship from Madagascar landed on the coast of South Carolina for repairs. The governor of the colony was gracious to the captain and his crew and assisted them in their repairs. As a token of his gratitude, the captain presented the governor with a bag of seed rice. South Carolina was the leading state in rice production for many years.

During the Industrial Age, man began experimenting with foodstuffs, including rice. Rice was milled and the outer bran layers were removed to reveal the beautiful, lustrous white kernel. Unfortunately, the resulting product is very low in food value. In areas of the world where rice was a major foodstuff, dreadful diseases began to result. When polished rice was introduced to Japan, beriberi soon became epidemic. The common people returned to the whole grain and health returned. Other nations were not so lucky, and many years of suffering resulted before they realized the problem.

Description

Between 7,000 and 8,000 different kinds of rice exist. Rice is a cereal grass and belongs in the same family as oats, barley, rye, and wheat, although it needs more moisture and warmth than these other grains.

Some varieties of rice depend upon flooding for growth, and others depend upon rainfall. Some types of rice grow only in one way, while others can adapt to various methods of farming. Most rice grown in the world today grows in flooded fields.

Brown rice has only the hull and a small amount of the bran removed. It retains more minerals, vitamins, and salts than highly processed polished rice. Brown rice is an excellent starch. Unpolished rice is balanced in composition and is nonfattening.

The three general classifications of rice are long grain, medium grain, and short (pearl) grain. Long grain rice keeps its beautiful, long, slender shape as it cooks. It cooks up very light and fluffy. Each kernel is separate. Long grain brown rice is the most expensive kind of rice as it has a tendency to break and the perfect, unbroken kernels bring a high price. Short grain brown rice creates moist grains that tend to cling to one another when cooked. They do not dry out easily; they are great to cook and hold over for the next meal. Short grain kernels are usually a fatter kernel.

All rice has essentially the same food value. The varying textures of cooked rice constitute the major difference as to choice. The known nutritive content of rice includes thiamin, riboflavin, niacin, carbohydrates, phosphorous, magnesium, calcium, potassium, silicon, sodium, fat, iron, and protein. Rice contains 1,633 calories per pound dry weight.

Uses

Rice is a high-yielding grain and requires little fuel for its preparation. These two features are of great importance in the overcrowded and underfueled areas of Asia.

Acceptable breads may be made from rice flour. Rice flour may be substituted for up to one-fourth of the wheat flour in a given recipe. In cookies and cakes, rice flour may be mixed with other grain flours. Rice in its various forms may be steamed or boiled, or used in casseroles, soups, curries, puddings, cakes, waffles, pilafs, and wine.

Home Grinding Procedures

Rice grinds very easily in either a stone grinder or the Magic Mill III Plus™.

Rye

History

Rye probably originated in southwest Asia, along with wheat, oats, and barley. Rye or *rie*, as it is sometimes spelled, is mentioned by name in the Bible. It also goes by the name **fitches**, which is an alternate name for black cummin, an aromatic seed used in cooking. More than likely, fitches was the name given to rye in one given area. The name **rye** evolved into the universal name.

Rye seed was brought to America by immigrants from Holland in the early 1800s. As the Dutch settlers migrated west, so did rye. The Dutch settled in Pennsylvania, but rye continued its westward trek with pioneering farmers.

Description

Rye is a nutritious grain ranking close to wheat in nutritional value. It has less fat than wheat and compares favorably with wheat and corn in protein and carbohydrate content. However, vitamin B 1 in rye is lower than in barley, wheat, and oats.

The nutritional elements in rye are thiamin, riboflavin, niacin, fat, silicon, iron, magnesium, unsaturated fatty acids, calcium, sodium, protein, phosphorous, potassium, carbohydrates, and vitamin E. Rye contains 1,515 calories per pound of dry weight.

Rye is not used as extensively as most other grains. In fact, the demand for rye is slowly decreasing as more and more people are using wheat, which makes a lighter textured bread. Dark rye flour comes from the grinding of whole rye. For lighter flour, the outer coats of the rye kernel are removed before grinding.

Production

Rye often grows where conditions are quite unfavorable for another type of crop. It can be found growing along many roadways, in weed patches, and in abandoned fields. The extreme cold and adverse soil conditions of northern Europe make it difficult for most cereal grains to flourish. Rye, however, has grown well under these conditions for centuries and has blessed northern Europe with its productivity. The civilizations of northern Europe owe their existence to this phenomenal grain. Rye has the greatest winter hardiness of all small grains and will grow in soil so infertile that no other grain will grow. It now extends to the Americas and as far north as the Arctic circle.

Rye also grows well in fertile soil, but since it is not a big money crop, fertile soil is usually reserved for higher paying crops. Because rye cross-pollinates easily, it is difficult to keep a pure strain. Consequently, only a few strains are known.

Uses

Rye has become a mainstay cereal grain in northern Europe and Asia. It is principally used for making breads, for feeding livestock, and for pasture.

The gluten in rye is inferior to that of wheat and does not have the elasticity needed for making light-textured breads. Breads made from rye are heavy and dark in color. Rye bread gets the name "black bread" from this color.

In the United States, rye is nearly always used with white wheat flour so as to give the rye flour lightness. Caraway seeds are also used; they give the unique flavor associated with rye bread. In some countries of Europe, a portion of the rye straw is pounded into a powder and used along with the grain in the making of bread. This procedure accounts for some of the coarseness.

Besides yeast breads, rye is also used in muffins, pancakes, cookies, and cakes. It makes a great cereal, either whole kernel or cracked. Casseroles and pilafs are also a good way to enjoy rye. Rye may be sprouted and used in salads and baking.

Rye is sometimes used as a pasture crop, taking the place of winter wheat, which is harvested rather early in the growing season. Like buckwheat, rye makes a good green manure crop. It improves the soil by adding nitrogen. It is sometimes planted in the spring and plowed under so a more valuable crop can be planted later. It is also planted as a cover crop for another grain to protect the young seedlings from the sun.

Home Grinding Procedures

Rye can usually be ground in a home stone mill. Because it is a softer kernel than wheat, feed it through the mill slowly and in small quantities. Rye absorbs moisture readily and may be a challenge as it may clog the pores of a stone mill. The Magic Mill III Plus™ mills rye into a fine flour with no problem.

Sorghum (Milo)

History

Sorghum is a grain native to tropical Africa and is its leading cereal grain. The first sorghum to come to the United States came from France, however. It was a Chinese variety, Chinese Amber, and arrived in 1855. In 1857, sixteen varieties were brought into the United States from Natal, South Africa.

Sorghum was found on the grocery shelves of America as late as World War I, but it disappeared from regular grocery markets after the war.

Description

Sorghum comes in a variety of types, and its uses range from broom straws to syrup. Its wide usage explains why sorghum is so universally grown. Depending on the type of sorghum, the pith may be juicy or dry. The leaves resemble corn leaves and are about 2 inches wide and 2½ feet long. The color of the grain may be white, yellow, red, or brown.

Sorghum is higher in protein and lower in fat than corn. The mineral composition differs only slightly from corn, and the vitamin content in grain sorghum is similar to white corn.

Sweet sorghum or sorgos has sweet, juicy stems and grows usually 6 to 14 feet tall, having loose panicles, drooping branches, and tall, red-brown spikelets. The seeds are small and bitter. This type of sorghum grows a heavier stock and is cultivated for the sweet juice found in the stalk, which is boiled down into sorghum syrup. Animal feed and silage can both be made from sweet sorghum.

Grain sorghums include kafir, durra, milo, maize, Egyptian corn, and African millet. Black Indian, Chinese, and pearl millet are also types of sorghum. Grain sorghum can grow 15 feet high. However, some plant breeders have developed plants that grow only 2 to 3 feet high, permitting harvesting with standard grain harvesters.

With nearly 95 percent of the nutritive value of corn, the seeds of grain sorghum are nutritionally valuable for all classes of livestock and poultry. Grain sorghums are excellent for forage. Farmers often feed the grain to livestock or make the entire plant into silage.

Grass sorghums, including sudan grass and tunis grass, are used for pasture and for forage. These annuals grow quickly and may reach heights of 10 feet. This type of sorghum makes excellent summer pasture. Johnson grass, a perennial sorghum and a pest when out of control, makes excellent cattle feed or hay.

Broom corn is a variety whose branches of the panicle are elongated and are thus adapted to the manufacture of whisk brooms. Sometimes seeds are still on the broom straws and may be planted.

Uses

The uses of sorghum are wide and varied. Pasturing cattle on the stubble of sorghum is common. For human consumption, sorghum is used as a grain and a syrup, depending on the type grown. In all countries except the United States, it is used extensively as a cereal food. The grain is ground into flour and used to make pancakes, porridge, and flatbreads. African wives and daughters spend up to two hours a day pounding sorghum grain into flour for their families. This time is a social hour for the women as they get together in one hut and sing or visit in rhythm to their pounding.

Sweet sorghum provides sweetening for food. It has long been an important sweetening agent in the eastern United States, especially in the Appalachian Mountains where grain sorghum is also extensively used.

Sorghum grain produces edible oil, starch, dextrose, paste, and alcoholic beverages. In some countries, the people chew the sweet stalk of the sorghum.

Home Grinding Procedures

Sorghum is very easily ground in most stone mills and in the Magic Mill III Plus™.

Wheat

History

The history of wheat and the history of man are closely related. Scientists believe that wheat was first cultivated between the Tigris and Euphrates rivers in an area called the Fertile Crescent.

Throughout recorded history, man has ground wheat to make his daily bread. The Egyptians, about 3000 B.C. began the practice of sifting the fine flour from the coarser pieces to get white flour. The procedure was very expensive, and only the royalty had the privilege of enjoying light, white breads.

The Hebrews were the first people to make a sourdough bread. Perhaps a young Hebrew woman forgot about a batch of bread in the making, and it soured. In baking the dough, however, it was discovered that the bread was lighter in texture. Whatever the origin, leavening had a dramatic impact on bread making.

In 500 B.C. the Greeks combined bakeries with flour mills. The Romans developed the process still further by establishing baking schools. A Roman baker was furnished with a house and was made exempt from the army, setting him up in society as an enviable person. These bakers developed the first union with their own set of rules.

Once a baker, always a baker, and this tradition continued. Bakers' children even had to marry other bakers' children. The bakers, in turn for all the notoriety, had to live up to the expectations of the people. If the quality of their bread was inferior, they were forced to walk the streets with their products around their necks. If their breads did not improve, rumor has it that they were sometimes baked in their own ovens! They also had to be sure of the poundage of their breads. In fear of the consequences, they would add another roll to a purchase, thus originating the "baker's dozen."

As man settled into towns and cities, grain became a basic part of the culture. Man learned to trade and barter. Wars were fought over wheat-producing lands. In fact, Hitler waited until the harvest was over to begin the drive against Poland. Napoleon's troops wept when they saw that the Russians had burned their grain fields; Napoleon had depended on that grain for his army's sustenance. The result—Napoleon lost the war. Marie Antoinette unwisely said of the starving French peasants, "Let them eat cake." The government fell, and she was beheaded. In World War I, the allies cut off the German food supplies. Herbert Hoover said, "The first word in war is spoken by guns—but the last word has always been spoken by bread."

As man has become more proficient at producing wheat for himself and his neighbor, much labor has been saved. One hundred years ago, more than sixty-four hours were required to prepare the soil, plant, and harvest one acre of wheat. Now, the same work takes less than three hours. In the early nineteenth century, four out of five men were needed to keep food on the nation's tables. Now, one out of twenty-eight produce our food.

Many attempts to develop superior new strains of wheat have taken place. One of the first successful achievements in this field was the development of the Marquis strain in Canada. This cross-pollination has been so successful that wheat can now be produced in virtually every country of the world.

Description and Uses

Wheat is the king of grains. It is the one grain whose prime purpose is to feed mankind. Some of the other grains are used principally by animals, and man enjoys them as an alternate grain in the diet. Some people store large quantities of wheat for a "rainy day," but wheat was not intended to be stored. Wheat was intended to be used to provide the nutritious elements needed to maintain strong bodies, clear minds, and healthy offspring.

In an alphabetical listing of grains, wheat is the last mentioned. Nevertheless, in the use of grains for human consumption, wheat ranks first for many reasons. It is the only grain with gluten in the proper texture to facilitate the rising of bread. Gluten, properly developed in the kneading process, traps the yeast gas in the bread dough and causes it to rise. With finely ground whole wheat, a beautiful, light loaf of bread is easily obtained.

Wheat also ranks first because of its nutritional value. Each whole kernel of wheat contains the germ, the bran, and the endosperm. When the wheat kernel is used in its entirety, the following nutrients are provided: thiamin, riboflavin, pyridozine, protein, pantothenic acid, niacin, barium, silver, inositol, folic acid, choline, vitamin E, boron, silicon, sodium, chlorine, calcium, iron, phosphorous, magnesium, potassium, manganese, copper, sulphur, iodine, and fluorine.

Wheat is the world's most important grain crop. The wheat grown annually, worldwide, would fill a freight train stretching nearly twice around the world. In the United States, each person eats about 126 pounds of wheat each year.

Five types of wheat are grown in the United States—hard winter wheat, hard spring wheat, soft spring wheat, white wheat, and durum.

Hard winter wheat is planted in the fall. It is usually dry-land wheat, grown without being watered, except by snow or rain. The extreme northern states are too cold for this type of wheat, but it grows well across Idaho, Montana, Oklahoma, and Kansas. Dry winters and springs make the protein content high, the moisture low. Hard winter wheat is a high volume producer.

Hard spring wheat is planted in the spring. Like hard winter wheat, it is not irrigated, thus yielding a high protein and low moisture content. This type of grain is quite expensive. It is usually mixed with hard winter wheat, a combination which makes an excellent loaf of bread.

Soft spring wheat has been irrigated. It usually has a larger yield than hard wheat but is lower in protein. It is principally used for stock feed. Soft spring wheat is also used in making cakes, cookies, pastries, or other baked goods that use baking powder, baking soda, or shortening as leavening.

White wheat is used to make crackers. It is also the best wheat to use when making rejuvelac, a fermented wheat water drink. Though other types of wheat may be used for this drink, white wheat gives a more delicate flavor.

Durum wheat is used for making macaroni, noodles, and all kinds of pasta.

Popular demand has caused the milling industry to produce up to 250 different grades of wheat flour. The more common ones are as follows:

Graham flour is coarsely milled whole wheat flour. It adds texture to the finished product, such as in graham crackers. Most of the time the germ has been removed.

Pastry flour is milled from soft, low protein wheat. The bran and germ have been removed. In some pastry flour, cornstarch has been added to give the flour the texture it needs for making light cakes. When grinding whole grain pastry flour at home, grind flour exceedingly fine and use 2 tablespoons barley flour, cornstarch, or arrowroot starch in place of 2 tablespoons of whole wheat flour in each cup of flour.

Enriched flour has been stripped of its bran and germ, and nutrients have been added back into the flour. An interesting history attends the origin of enriched flour. Until the nineteenth century, the use of white flour was confined to royalty or to the wealthy people who could afford it. In Paris in 1876, the first light, white French rolls were exhibited. The governor of Minnesota was in attendance at the exposition and determined that America must have the "benefits" of this discovery. He learned how to separate the various components of the grain to achieve the white flour he

desired. He came back to America and developed the steel roller mills which accelerated the grinding of grain into flour.

This product contained no wheat germ oil. It did not become rancid. Volumes could be ground and transported nationwide. This new process put all the local stone-grinding mills out of business. This white flour became a status symbol, and light, white bread became the objective of virtually every homemaker. Few people thought about the bran, germ, wheat oil, and other nutrients that had been eliminated.

Illnesses relating to nutrition began to be more prevalent, and the cause was found to be the removal of the life-giving qualities from grains. When beriberi, pellagra, and anemia reared their ugly heads, the milling industry was asked to return the flour to its original form. The markets that the millers had procured for the "milled away" portions of the grain were so lucrative, however, that the millers refused to return to selling milled grain in its whole state. Instead, they added one mineral, iron, and three B vitamins, niacin, thiamin, and riboflavin, to enrich the white flour.

Although all-purpose flour in America is nearly always enriched, it has only a fraction of the food value of the whole wheat kernel. Over thirty nutrients are known to exist in the wheat kernel, and most of them are removed in the milling process. This flour, which is principally the endosperm of the grain, is nearly always bleached, and it contains none of the roughage inherent in the wheat kernel—roughage essential for adding bulk to the diet. Some bakeries add cellulose or sawdust to the bread to replace the bran and wheat germ that has been removed and given to the animal food industry. The term **enriched** can certainly be misleading.

Commercially ground whole wheat flour contains most of the bran, but the wheat germ and germ oil have been removed to prevent the flour from becoming rancid. These two ingredients contain the elements that are the life force of the grain and are essential for good health. Whole wheat flour should be ground as needed. Freshly ground flour contains all the nutrients found in the whole grain without the preservatives.

Gluten flour is commercially made from white flour. To extract the gluten, flour and enough water to make a soft dough are kneaded until the dough is rubbery and elastic. The dough is then washed, rinsing away the starch and leaving a rubbery mass of concentrated high protein. This protein is then dried and ground into flour. Adding several tablespoons of gluten flour to bread gives a lighter texture. Adding gluten flour to a multigrain bread permits the use of a wider variety of grains that would otherwise make a loaf heavy in texture.

Much of the bran and wheat germ is washed away when making gluten from whole wheat flour. Whole wheat gluten is often made into "wheatmeat." This meat substitute may be flavored with bouillon, onion, or soy sauce. Steaks or hamburger-type meats are the most satisfactory end products. This book does not dwell on gluten, as gluten is only a portion of the wheat. The focus is on adding grains to the diet, rather than using a portion of the grains.

In addition to wheat flour, wheat is available in these forms:

Bulgur wheat is wheat that has been cracked, parboiled, dried, and partially debranned for later use. It tastes somewhat like wild rice.

Cracked wheat is simply wheat that has been cracked. It may be used instead of bulgur in any given recipe.

Wheat meal is wheat that has been milled to the texture of cornmeal.

Production

Somewhere every month of the year, a crop of wheat is harvested. It can grow in areas of less than 12 inches of rainfall a year and in areas of up to 70 inches per year. It can be grown from the Arctic circle to the equator and from below sea level to 10,000 foot elevations. About 70 percent of the world's cultivated ground grows cereal grains. Wheat amounts to 22 percent and rice is second with 13 percent. The prairies of the United States, Canada, and Russia are excellent soils for wheat.

Home Grinding Procedures

When purchasing wheat, check the moisture and protein content of the wheat. High protein wheat is necessary for good quality breads. Low moisture is necessary so that when the grain is ground and the moisture is released, the flour does not build up inside the cabinet and glaze the stones of a home stone mill. When the motor begins to heat up and the grain ceases to feed through the grinder, moisture has built up. Should this occur, open the stones as widely as they will go and grind the remainder of the grain, if possible. Open the cabinet to allow the moisture to escape and the stones to cool. Do not close the stones again until they are cool. Moisture and flour make paste, and the stones may glue together if they are left in the fine grind position. Grinding a little popcorn in the mill will usually remove the glazing.

Moisture may be released from the grain prior to grinding by placing the wheat in a warm 150° F. oven for about an hour. Leave the oven door ajar.

Moisture is not a problem with the Magic Mill III Plus™. Wheat with a high moisture content (10 percent or above) goes through the mill a little more slowly, but because there is no grinding surface, glazing is no longer a problem.

Triticale (A Wheat Derivative)

History

The word **triticale** comes from the scientific names of wheat (triticum) and rye (secale). Scientists have been trying for years to produce a grain that combines the hardiness of rye with the gluten qualities of wheat and that has a high yield. In 1937, they produced a grain which was partially fertile and came close to their goal. Experiments have continued, and the Golden Kernel 707 (triticale) is one such variety. Over 2,000 such grains have been produced, but not all of them retain the characteristics the scientists have been working for.

Description

Triticale seems to be a desirable grain. It is exceptionally high in protein (usually about 17 percent) and thus is valuable as a stock feed. Triticale is a larger kernel than wheat and is a little darker in color.

Uses

Triticale makes excellent pastries and may be used where regular wheat is used, except in bread. Because triticale protein adapted more of the characteristics of rye than wheat, bread made with it is more dense than wheat bread. Add a vitamin C tablet and 2 tablespoons of lecithin when used in bread. These additions will help the texture of the bread. The cellular structure of triticale cannot handle more than one rising when making bread of 100 percent triticale. Shape the bread and put it in the greased pans immediately. Allow it to rise only once, and bake it. Using two-thirds wheat flour and one-third triticale flour improves the quality of bread.

Triticale also makes an excellent cereal, cracked or whole kernel. It may be used in casseroles where rice or cracked wheat is used.

Triticale sprouts beautifully. These sprouts are enjoyable as a snack food or in salads.

Home Grinding Procedures

Triticale grinds very well in either a stone mill or the Magic Mill III Plus™.

From the bounteous bread basket tumble: (clockwise from far left) Pumpkin-Oatmeal Bread (page 28), Multigrain Bread baked in a fluted brioche pan (page 29), Black Russian Rye Bread (page 33), French Bread (page 23), Rye-Wheat Bread sprinkled with sesame seeds (page 30), and Buttermilk-Cracked Wheat rolls (page 27). Other shaped rolls and breadsticks hail from Ezekiel Bread (page 29), Best-ever Magic Mill Bread (page 22), or a braided combination of the two.

Yeast Breads

The art of baking bread is nearly as old as the history of mankind. Methods of grinding grains and combining them to make bread have developed as man has gained skill and experience. The product which began with essentially liquid and some type of grain flour has evolved to include yeast, salt, and usually a little sweetener. Other ingredients, such as eggs, shortening, and herbs, have been added to suit individual preferences. Each addition gives flavor, improves texture, or adds variety to the bread.

The first leavening used in breads was airborne yeasts. This method can still be used to make sourdough starter. The distinctive flavor and method of making sourdough is very much a part of today's baking. For centuries, people did not understand what made the sourdough starter raise bread, but they liked the results. In 1877, Pasteur explained this wonder, and commercial yeasts began to be produced. Now, homemakers have the convenience of yeast in dry or cake form, as well as carefully nurtured sourdough starter. A variety of grain flours is also available, and with these ingredients, breads of all textures, tastes, and shapes can be produced at home.

Basic Ingredients in Yeast Bread

The **liquid** in yeast breads may range from water, milk, and potato water to fruit juice, buttermilk, yogurt, cottage cheese, whey, and bouillon. Liquids used in yeast breads should be sufficiently warm so that after the sweetening and shortening are added, the temperature of the combination is body temperature or slightly above (106 to 110° F). Whole milk should be scalded and cooled to body temperature. Hot water and powdered milk combinations do not need to be scalded.

The **sweetening** used for yeast breads can be honey, molasses, applesauce, fruit juice, or sugar. However, diastatic malt, malt syrup, and dried fruits are beginning to find a place as sweetening agents in breads. The amount of sweetening changes from recipe to recipe. Some breads use no sweetening at all, such as in French breads, some whole wheat breads, and sourdough breads.

Sugarless breads are tasty, especially when made with diastatic malt, malt syrup, or whey. These ingredients may be used in any bread recipe to replace another sweetening agent.

Yeast is a living organism that grows in the presence of moisture and carbohydrates and at a warm temperature (106 to 110° F). Under these conditions, the yeast ferments, forming gases. These gases are captured by the rubbery gluten in wheat flour. Like tiny balloons, they cause the bread to raise.

Commercial yeast comes in a moist cake or dry granules. Either form is excellent. However, all commercial yeasts are not the same. Quality can vary. If there is a concern about yeast quality, pour a little sweetener and the required amount of yeast into ½ cup warm water. Two tablespoons of top-quality yeast will fill a cup with froth in 5 to 7 minutes. Increase the yeast quantity in the bread if the yeast is slow. Granulated yeast should be kept in a covered container in a cool place and used within a six-month period. Yeast can be stored in the freezer and used as needed. A moist yeast cake will store in the refrigerator for about one week.

Shortening in yeast breads may be oil, shortening, lard, butter, margarine, bacon grease, or animal fat. Shortening makes bread tender and rich. Dough made without shortening tends to be sticky, and the bread is drier and heavier. Butter is particularly delicious when used in breads.

Salt helps bring out the flavor of the bread. However, salt may be replaced by herbs, sea salt, or eliminated completely. Although the texture and shape of bread is not affected by the omission of salt, the elimination substantially alters the flavor.

The **flour** used in yeast breads varies greatly. The most common type used in the United States is all-purpose enriched flour. However, whole wheat flour, freshly ground, is becoming popular in many homes. The types of wheat flour are discussed at the front of this book. Any of the bread recipes contained herein may have the whole wheat flour content altered with white flour in a 1:2 ratio or 1:1 ratio, according to your your family's taste.

Rye flour is also a favorite. Breads made with rye flour are dense. Wheat flour is often added to make rye breads lighter.

Other grain flours may be used for their distinctive flavors. However, they tend to make bread heavy as they have no gluten to help lift the dough. Replace no more than one-fourth of the flour content in a given recipe with variety grain flours. While it is not a grain, soy flour from milled soybeans is added to bread to increase the protein content and to improve the texture. Exchange 1 cup of soy flour for 1 cup of flour in a 12-cup flour batch. Protein content increases by 40 percent.

Sunflower seeds, sesame seeds, nuts, raisins, and sprouts contribute texture and flavor when added to dough. Sprouts in dough may require a longer baking time.

Bread Making Tips

When making whole grain breads, use 1 table-spoon of yeast for each 4 cups of whole grain flour. Whole grain breads need the extra boost the added yeast gives. If your whole grain bread recipe results in heavy loaves, try these tips for a 12-cup flour batch:

The addition of one vitamin C tablet and/or 2 tablespoons lecithin (oil or granulated) helps strengthen the cell walls of the dough and make the bread lighter. Vitamin C tablets should be at least 150 milligrams. Add the vitamin C to the warm liquid so it can dissolve. Two tablespoons lemon juice may be used instead of the vitamin C tablet. One-half cup soybeans milled into flour may replace the lecithin.

For lightness, add 5 to 6 tablespoons gluten flour to the flour. Gluten flour may be purchased at health food stores. Similar results are achieved by the addition of 4 tablespoons dough-pep, available at some health food stores. Magic Mill dealers sell Dough Enhancer, an excellent additive to breads.

Check yeast for activity. Yeast may be proofed in the entire water content of the recipe or in ½ cup warm water.

Bread dough should be as pliable and soft as possible but not sticky. Adjust flour content accordingly. The protein and moisture content of the wheat plus the humidity in the air will slightly alter the amount of flour needed in any recipe.

Try kneading the bread and allowing it to rest for an hour or more before shaping it into loaves. Resting the dough improves the texture and quality of the bread.

When kneading bread by hand, it may be convenient to use a large dishpan. Gauge the amount of flour used in the kneading process so that when the dough has been kneaded and the proper texture is obtained, the bowl is cleaned of all excess dough. To remove any remaining dough from the pan, use a tablespoon or more of flour, and roll it along where the dough is clinging to the pan. The flour will collect the bits of dough. Knead this little bit of dough into the bread dough. Oil the bread, and place it back into the cleaned dishpan to raise.

A loaf splitting along the pan as it bakes may have several possible causes. The dough may contain too much flour; try reducing the flour content. The quality of the wheat may be a contributing factor. Rolling the dough on a lightly greased surface may prevent drying during the raising process. If the bread still splits, try putting a pan of hot water in the bottom of the oven, and bake the bread in a very hot oven, 400 to 450° F. High heat kills the yeast almost immediately, and the bread will not raise any more. An incorrect baking temperature may also cause the loaf to split.

If it becomes evident that something is wrong with a batch of bread which isn't raising properly, don't bake it. Go back over the recipe and analyze the problem. If more yeast is needed, dissolve 2 to 3 tablespoons of yeast in ½ cup warm water. Reknead this liquid into the raw dough in the mixer. Add more flour to bring the dough back to the proper texture. Reshape the bread, let it raise, and bake it.

The baking process may be likened to fruit ripening. The process changes the starch, which is difficult to digest, into a sugar which is easily assimilated into the body.

Bread Pans

The size of pans used in baking bread is important. Often homemakers complain that their bread tastes great, but it doesn't look like it should. The cosmetic appearance of bread is affected by the depth and width of the pans.

The width of the pan makes a big difference. The 9 x 5-inch pan is too wide to give a whole-grain loaf a beautifully rounded top. However, if a 9 x 5-inch pan is the only size available, shape two softball-size balls of dough into loaves and put one at each end of the pan. These two smaller loaves will have a better cosmetic appearance.

A loaf baked in a three-pound shortening can yields large round slices of bread for open-faced sandwiches. Fill the can a little over one-third full with dough, and let it raise to within 1 inch of the top of the can before baking.

Another good bread pan is a 46-ounce juice can. When you want to give someone something special, make a batch of bread and bake a loaf in this "Good Neighbor" can. The loaf can be delivered in the can itself. Grease the sides and bottom of the can with shortening or a lecithin oil/salad oil combination. Use a softball-size piece of bread dough, and shape it into a round loaf. Drop into the greased can. The dough should fill the can almost 2½ inches. Allow the dough to raise to within 1 inch of the top of the can.

It is not necessary to wash bread pans after each use. Wipe them clean with a paper towel. When it becomes necessary to wash them, do it immediately after use and turn them upside-down in a warm oven to dry. This procedure prevents rusting.

To estimate the pan size and weight of a loaf, follow this simple guideline: One cup of liquid in a recipe makes about one pound of bread.

Pan sizes	Bread weight
5 x 2½ inches	¾ pound
7½ x 3½ inches	1 pound
8½ x 4½ inches	1½ pounds
9 x 5 inches	2 pounds
46-ounce can	1 pound
3-pound shortening can	1½ pounds

Shaping of Bread

When the dough has been kneaded, pour all the dough out onto an oiled surface and measure off loaves. Start by shaping the dough which was measured off first, allowing the other portions time to relax, thus making it easier to handle.

Loaf Pan

To grease bread pans, use a vegetable oil spray; hard, unsalted shortening; or 1 part liquid lecithin and 2 parts salad oil. Sprinkle greased bread pans with rolled oats or cornmeal to give a different texture to the crust.

After the dough has been divided into loaf-size portions, take one portion and pull it out to about 12 inches in length. Slap it hard on a greased kneading surface. Using your fingers, flatten and stretch it to a 9 x 12-inch rectangle. Fold the dough in thirds lengthwise. Flatten it out again to a 9 x 12-inch rectangle. This time, fold the dough into thirds widthwise. Finally, press the dough out to a rectangle the length of the bread pan and about 6 inches in width. Roll up, starting at the long edge. Seal the edges and the ends by pressing together. Place in a greased pan, seam-side down. If the loaf is slightly longer than the pan, lift the dough in the center. Let both ends fit into the ends of the greased loaf pan. The center will settle into the pan.

French Bread Loaf

Divide the dough into loaf-size portions. Using one portion of dough, pull it out to about 12 inches in length. Grasping the ends of the bread, slap it onto a greased surface. With your fingers, flatten and shape the dough into a 10-inch square. Beginning at one corner, roll the dough diagonally, creating an oblong loaf with the center larger than the ends. Tuck under the ends. Place seam side down on a greased baking sheet that has been sprinkled with cornmeal. Brush the top of the loaf with a beaten egg white or an egg wash made of 1 egg yolk and 1 tablespoon milk. Sprinkle generously with sesame seeds, and diagonally slash across the top three to four times with a

sharp knife. Cover, and let raise at room temperature until double in bulk. Bake according to the directions on the recipe.

Round Loaf

Using a loaf-size portion, hold one end of the dough and slap the rest on a greased surface. Fold the portion held in your hand into the dough, and slap it hard again. Repeat two or three times until the dough is formed into a raindrop shape. Finally, tuck under the pointed end, and place the folded end down on a greased baking sheet.

Turtle Buns

Shape the round body of the turtle from a piece of dough about 3 inches in diameter and ½ inch in width. Let the children shape four fat 1½-inch legs, a pointed tail, and a 1½-inch head. Gently lift the sides of the body and position the turtle's appendages slightly underneath. With a pair of kitchen shears, split the ends of the legs into two toes. Give the turtle a big smile by snipping the dough with a pair of scissors, and insert a small piece of foil to hold the mouth open. Snip the eyes and insert foil. Finally, snip all over the back of the turtle, making it rough in texture. Let the bread raise, and bake. The turtle body makes a hamburger bun.

Dogilator

Shape a piece of dough ½-inch thick, 6-inches long, and 1½-inches wide. Let the children roll out four legs. Unlike turtle legs, these legs should be slender and shaped like a backward S. Lift the sides of the alligator and gently position legs. With a pair of kitchen shears, cut into the dough a third of the way to give the animal a big smile. Insert foil to hold the mouth open. Snip eyes and insert foil. Snip the back with scissors to give a rough appearance. Let the bread raise, and bake. To insert a hot dog, extend the alligator's smile to his tail with a sharp knife.

Dough Decorating

Dough sculpting gives character to breads and creates some beautiful masterpieces. Follow the directions given for shaping the dough into a round or French loaf, and position the dough on the pan. Be sure dough is well oiled. Follow one of the patterns below for decorating.

Wheat

Roll a small piece of dough into a long, slender strip. Position on loaf. Shape and position two more strips of unequal length. Using kitchen shears, cut nearly through the stem, and with your scissors gently pull the cut portion out from the strip. Alternate cuts

Children delight in Turtle and Dogilator hamburger and hot dog buns. Simple bread decorating (shown with wheat mot turns an ordinary loaf into a spectacular creatic

on one side and then the other for about one-third the way down each stem.

Rose

Shape enough dough for a loaf of bread into a raindrop shape. In the center of the wide end, cut out a small circle of dough the size of a marble. Shape the dough into a ball, and replace it in the hole. With kitchen shears, make five V-shape cuts into the dough, and with your scissors, lift each up to form petals around the ball. Make five more slightly larger V-shape cuts around the first row, lifting each petal. Repeat for a third row. Roll a small piece of dough into a rope to make a stem. Position one end under the last row of rose petals, and lay the stem gracefully down the center of the raindrop, ending at the point. Cut into the stalk to form thorns. Shape a leaf of dough, cut indentations along the sides, and position on stem. Make veins with the point of the scissors. Let dough raise, and bake. Brush with melted butter.

Grape Cluster

Roll the stem in same manner as you would for a wheat stalk. Position the stem on loaf. Split each end with your scissors to make a V. Shape the leaves as for a rose. Roll small pieces of dough into ½-inch balls. Position in clusters over and around the stem. Finally, roll a thin strip of dough and coil to resemble the vine. Work quickly so that the sculpting can raise with the bread. Brush with melted butter after baking.

Raising of Bread

Allowing dough to raise in the bowl before shaping creates a lighter loaf. This raising may be from one to three hours. After shaping the bread, set a kitchen timer during the final raising. Bread that has raised too high before baking either falls or is coarse and crumbly. If the dough has raised too long, reshape it, replace it in the pan, and let it raise once more.

There are several methods for helping bread to raise. The most common is to cover it with a dish towel and allow it to raise on a counter in a draft-free area. An alternate method is to place the bread in the oven over a pan of hot water. Turn on the oven light for added warmth.

Bread may be raised in an oven preheated to 200° F. Turn the oven off, position the pans so that air can circulate, and set the timer. Thirty minutes is usually long enough. If the bread is not quite raised, turn the oven on to 150° F. for an additional 5 to 10 minutes. This added heat gives the yeast an extra boost. Finally, set the recommended baking temperature, and bake as directed.

Free-formed loaves (loaves that are shaped and placed on a baking sheet) should be allowed to raise only at room temperature. Free-formed loaves will flatten if raised in a warm oven.

Specialty Breads

When making bread, it is easy to achieve several different flavors from the same dough. Here are some suggestions:

Swedish Roll

Roll a loaf-size piece of dough into a rectangle. Spread with melted butter, cinnamon, brown sugar, or a selection of nuts or seeds. Roll up as you would for cinnamon rolls. Place the entire roll on a greased baking sheet. Using a pair of kitchen shears, cut the roll into ½-inch slices, but do not cut all the way to the bottom of the roll. Pull the first slice gently to the right side of the pan, and lay it so that the cut side is up. Lay the second slice on the left side of the roll, cut side up. The rolls are connected by the section of dough along the bottom of the roll, and each succeeding roll is laid on the bottom half of the roll preceding it. Continue the pattern, alternating the rolls on each side. Let raise until double, and bake 25 to 30 minutes in a 350° F. oven. Frost with powdered sugar icing, and decorate with maraschino cherries and nuts. The roll may also be placed on a greased pizza pan and shaped into a circle.

Cinnamon Swirl

Divide the dough into loaf-size portions. In one portion, mix a few raisins into the dough. Roll the dough out to the length of the bread pan, 6-inches wide, and ½-inch thick. Sprinkle with sugar and cinnamon. Nuts, sunflower seeds, and dried fruits are also good. Roll up lengthwise, and pinch seams together. Roll back and forth a few times to further seal the edges, keeping the roll pan length. Place in a well-greased bread pan, seam side down. Let raise, and bake as directed.

Cinnamon Rolls

Follow the instructions for Cinnamon Swirl. Instead of placing the dough in a bread pan, cut the loaf into cinnamon rolls. Bake on a greased cookie sheet or in a 9 x 9-inch baking dish. Frost while warm.

Onion-Cheese Bread

Roll out a loaf-size portion as directed for Cinnamon Swirl. Sprinkle with dehydrated onions, Parmesan cheese, and a little oregano. Roll up and place on a well-greased baking sheet that has been sprinkled with cornmeal. Brush with an egg white that has been mixed with 1 teaspoon of water. Sprinkle with sesame seeds, and slash the surface diagonally three or four times.

Mock Rye Bread

Roll out a loaf-size portion of dough as in the previous instructions. Sprinkle with 1 tablespoon caraway seed and 1 teaspoon anise seed. Roll up as you would for the Cinnamon Swirl, and place in a greased loaf pan.

Prune-Nut Swirl

Use dried prunes that have been stewed. Cut into small pieces. Generously sprinkle prunes over a loaf-size portion of dough that has been rolled out to a 9 x 12-inch rectangle. Add chopped nuts. Roll up as for Cinnamon Swirl. Pinch ends, and place seam-side down in a loaf pan. Let raise in a warm place, and bake according to recipe instructions.

Pizza Crust

Either with a rolling pin or with your fingers, roll out a loaf-size portion for a pizza crust. Position on a pizza pan, and partially bake for 5 minutes in a 450° F. oven before adding pizza toppings.

Whole Wheat Crackers

Spread sesame seeds on a lightly oiled surface, and roll a loaf-size portion of dough over the seeds until the dough is paper-thin. Turn the dough over onto a greased baking sheet, and trim to fit pan. Prick all over with a fork. Let the dough rest for 45 minutes, and bake in 350° F. oven for 10 minutes until crisp and golden. Break into pieces.

Biscuits

Cut biscuits from one loaf-size portion, bake on a lightly greased sheet, and serve hot. Biscuits may also be frozen raw and baked later in the week. When defrosting raw dough, remove from the freezer the day before and place in the refrigerator to defrost. Bring the dough to room temperature, let rise, and bake. Dough may be frozen for up to a week before baking.

Seasoned Bread Rounds

Using an unsweetened bread dough, break off golf ball-size pieces of dough. Place the balls about 7 inches apart on greased baking sheets and flatten into 6-inch circles. Brush with melted butter and top with shredded cheese, minced onions, poppy seeds, caraway seeds, sesame seeds, or cinnamon and brown sugar. Let rise for 30 minutes, and bake in a 350° F. oven for 10 minutes

Breadsticks

Make breadsticks from your favorite bread dough by pinching off small portions of dough and rolling out a little fatter than a pencil. Roll dough over a bed of sesame seeds, if desired. Bake in a 350° F. oven until lightly browned. Turn off oven and let breadsticks dry in the oven.

Best-ever Magic Mill Bread

Almost a slice of heaven! Thank you to Magic Mill distributor Joan Phillips in Mesa, Arizona.

Wheat

4	cups hot water, 110-115° F.
¼	cup honey
500	ml vitamin C
2	tablespoons yeast
¼	cup oil
2	tablespoons lecithin
½	cup nonfat dry powdered milk
½	cup whey
1½	tablespoons salt
10-12	cups whole wheat flour

Pour hot water, honey, and vitamin C into Bosch bowl. Add yeast, and allow to activate. Add oil, lecithin, powdered milk, whey, and salt. Mix in 6 cups flour, and knead 2 to 3 minutes. Add 4 to 5 cups additional flour, and knead for 10 minutes. At the end of the kneading time, dough should pull away from the sides of bowl. If dough clings, add a little more flour. Well grease four 7½ x 3½ x 2-inch bread pans. Remove dough from bowl, and divide into four equal portions. Shape into loaves. Place into greased pans, and allow to rise until double. Bake in a 350° F. oven for 45 minutes or until bread is well browned and sounds hollow when tapped. Remove from pans, and cool on wire racks. Makes 4 loaves.

Whole Wheat Bread

A terrific basic bread from the kitchen of Allen and Jeannine Burt, Magic Mill distributors in Portland, Oregon.

Wheat

5	cups warm water
⅓	cup honey
⅓	cup blackstrap molasses
3	tablespoons dry yeast
1½	tablespoons salt
⅔	cup oil
10-12	cups whole wheat flour

Pour warm water into Bosch mixing bowl. Add honey and molasses. Sprinkle yeast over water, and let activate. Add salt, oil, and whole wheat flour. Mix well. Knead 10 to 12 minutes. Divide into four equal portions, and shape into loaves. Place in well-greased 8½ x 4½ x 2½-inch bread pans. Place pans in a warm oven, and allow to rise until almost double and well crowned, approximately 25 minutes. Set oven temperature to 350° F. and turn on oven. Do not preheat. Bake 30 to 40 minutes. Makes 4 loaves.

Cracked Wheat Bread

Add 1 cup finely cracked wheat. Decrease flour.

Sprouted Wheat Bread

Sprout wheat kernels 2 to 3 days. Add 2 cups of sprouts. Increase flour as needed.

Sourdough Bread

Wheat

1	cup warm water
2	tablespoons yeast
1½	teaspoons salt
1	cup Sourdough Starter (below)
3	tablespoons molasses
3-4	cups whole wheat flour
2	cups all-purpose flour

Combine warm water, yeast, and salt in Bosch mixing bowl, Allow yeast to activate. Add Sourdough starter, molasses, and 3 cups whole wheat flour. Mix well. Add the all-purpose flour and enough of the remaining whole wheat flour to cause dough to pull away from the sides of the bowl. Knead 10 to 12 minutes. Divide in half, and shape into two loaves. Place in two well-greased 7½ x 3½ x 2-inch loaf pans. Cover, and allow to rise until double. Bake in a 350° F. oven for 45 minutes. Remove from pans, and cool on wire racks. Makes 2 loaves.

Sourdough Starter

1½	cups rye or wheat flour
1½	cups warm water
1	tablespoon yeast

Combine ingredients in a 2-quart glass jar. Cover, and let sour at room temperature for 2 to 3 days. Use 1 to 2 cups of starter as directed in recipes. Refrigerate the balance. Prior to using starter again, replenish the evening before with 1½ cups flour and 1½ cups water. For maximum flavor, use every 7 to 10 days. Starter improves as it is properly replenished and aged.

French Bread
Wheat

    2 **tablespoons yeast**
2½ **cups warm water**
   ¼ **cup honey**
   ½ **cup butter or margarine, melted**
2½ **teaspoons salt**
   4 **cups whole wheat flour**
3-3½ **cups all-purpose flour**
   ½ **cup water**
   1 **teaspoon cornstarch**
     Sesame seeds

Soften yeast in 1 cup of the warm water. Combine remaining 1½ cups warm water, honey, butter or margarine, and salt. Add yeast mixture and whole wheat flour. Knead to combine. Add enough all-purpose flour to cause dough to clean the sides of the bowl. Knead 10 minutes. Cover, and let rest for 10 minutes. Repeat kneading and resting procedure four more times. Transfer dough to a lightly floured surface, and divide into two equal portions. Shape into French-style loaves, and place on greased baking sheets. Brush with a glaze made of ½ cup water and cornstarch. Sprinkle with sesame seeds. Using a sharp knife, slash tops of loaves diagonally. Let rise until nearly double. To achieve a crusty, French-bread texture, heat oven to 400° F. Place a pan of boiling water on the floor of the oven. Allow to steam for 20 minutes before baking bread. Bake bread for 25 minutes. Makes 2 loaves.

English Muffin Bread
Corn, wheat

1⅓ **cups warm water**
   2 **tablespoons yeast**
   2 **tablespoons honey or molasses**
1½ **teaspoons salt**
   ⅓ **cup oil**
   2 **eggs**
3-4 **cups whole wheat flour**
     Cornmeal

Measure water, yeast, and honey or molasses into Bosch bowl. Allow time for yeast to activate. Add salt, oil, eggs, and whole wheat flour. Knead for 10 to 12 minutes. Cover, and let rise until double. Divide dough into two equal portions. Let rest. Grease the sides and bottoms of two 46-ounce cans, and dust

with cornmeal. Shape each portion of dough into a smooth ball, and drop into a can. Cover, and let rise until dough is about 1 inch from the top of the can. Bake in a 375°F. oven for 25 minutes. When bread is almost completely cooled, invert can and shake out bread. Makes 2 loaves.

> NOTE: All-purpose flour may be substituted for the whole wheat flour, or 2 cups all-purpose flour may be used in place of 2 cups whole wheat flour.

English Muffins

Prepare dough as for English Muffin Bread. Roll out on a lightly greased surface to ½-inch thickness. Cut with a 3-inch biscuit or cookie cutter. Dip dough in cornmeal, and bake on a lightly greased griddle at 275° F. for 8 to 10 minutes on each side, turning only once. Makes about 12.

Sprouted Wheat Bread
Wheat

2 **cups warm water**
2 **tablespoons yeast**
2 **cups sprouted wheat**
2½ **teaspoons salt**
5-7 **cups whole wheat flour**

Combine water, yeast, and sprouted wheat in Bosch mixing bowl. Allow yeast to activate. Add salt and flour. Mix well. Knead 10 to 12 minutes. Shape into two loaves, and place in well-greased 8½ x 4½ x 2½-inch pans. Let rise until nearly double. Bake in a 350° F. oven for 45 minutes. Makes 2 loaves.

> NOTE: For a sweeter bread, add 4 tablespoons molasses and 4 tablespoons oil.

Two-tone Bread

A beautiful bread that's very versatile. Children love to take it to school for lunch, and it's a guaranteed hit with guests.

Wheat

WHITE DOUGH:

- 3 cups warm water
- ⅓ cup honey
- 2 tablespoons yeast
- ⅓ cup oil
- 1¼ tablespoons salt
- 1 cup dry powdered milk
- 7-8 cups all-purpose flour

WHEAT DOUGH:

- 3 cups warm water
- ⅓ cup molasses
- 2 tablespoons yeast
- ⅓ cup oil
- 1¼ tablespoons salt
- 1 cup dry powdered milk
- 5-5½ cups whole wheat flour
- 2-2½ cups all-purpose flour

To prepare white dough, pour warm water into Bosch mixing bowl. Add honey. Sprinkle yeast over water, and let activate. Add oil, salt, powdered milk and flour. Mix well. Knead 7 minutes. Shape dough into a ball and transfer to a slightly greased bowl. Cover, and let rest while preparing whole wheat dough.

To prepare wheat dough, pour warm water into Bosch bowl. Add molasses, and sprinkle yeast over water. Allow yeast to activate. Add the remaining ingredients, and mix well. Knead 12 minutes.

To form loaves, divide the white dough into four equal portions. Divide the wheat dough into four portions. On an oiled surface, roll one portion of each into a 14 x 8 x ½-inch rectangle. Position whole wheat dough on top of white dough. Roll up, beginning with the 8-inch side. Press ends and edges of dough together to seal. Roll dough back and forth two or three times to further seal edges. Repeat procedure with remaining white and whole wheat dough. Place in four well-greased 8½ x 4½ x 2½-inch bread pans, and let rise until nearly double. Bake in 350° F. oven for 45 minutes. Remove bread from pans, and cool on wire racks. Makes 4 loaves.

Mock Rye Bread

Sprinkle a generous teaspoon of caraway seeds on each 14 x 8 x ½-inch rectangle of dough. Roll, and bake as directed for Two-tone Bread.

Cinnamon Swirl

Generously sprinkle each 14 x 8 x ½-inch rectangle of dough with brown sugar and cinnamon. Add nuts, seeds or raisins, if desired. Roll, and bake as directed for Two-tone Bread.

Brown and White Bubble Bread

Using half of the white dough and half of the wheat dough for Two-tone Bread, pinch off small pieces. Dip in melted butter, and roll in a cinnamon and sugar mixture. Place in a well-greased angel food or bundt pan. Generously sprinkle nuts and raisins among the dough balls. Fill pan half full. Let rise until nearly double. Bake in a 350° F. oven for 45 minutes. Remove from pan, and cool on a wire rack. Drizzle with powdered sugar frosting, and top with chopped nuts.

Triple Challah

Divide off one softball-size portion of white dough, and set aside. Divide off two softball-size portions of wheat dough. Roll out one whole wheat portion into a large rectangle. Sprinkle with caraway and anise seeds, and roll back up into a ball. Cut off two-thirds of each softball-size portion, and roll into a rope 18 inches in length. Loosely braid on a well-greased baking sheet. Sprinkle with sesame seeds. Make an 18-inch rope from each remaining one-third portion. Braid loosely, and center on top of the first braid. Combine 1 egg yolk and 1 tablespoon water, and brush bread. Sprinkle generously with sesame seeds or poppy seeds. Let rise until double. Bake in a 400° F. oven for 10 minutes, and then reduce heat to 350° F. and bake an additional 30 minutes.

Two-tone Bread pleases children and adults alike with its excellent flavor and eye appeal.

Creamed Corn Bread

No sweetening and no oil.

Wheat

       1   **16-ounce can cream-style corn**
       3   **cups hot water**
       3   **tablespoons yeast**
     1½   **tablespoons salt**
    8-10   **cups whole wheat flour**
           Cornmeal

Combine corn and water in Bosch mixing bowl. Add yeast, and allow to activate. Mix in salt and whole wheat flour. Knead 10 to 12 minutes. Grease five 46-ounce juice cans, and sprinkle with cornmeal. Divide dough into five equal portions. Shape into balls, and drop one in each can. Let rise until double. Bake in 350° F. oven for 40 minutes. Makes 5 loaves.

> NOTE: Whole kernel corn or reconstituted dried corn may be slightly pureed in the blender and used in place of the creamed corn.

Challah

> In early Jewish history, the local rabbi was supported by the people he served. When the Jewish homemaker made bread, a tenth of it was donated to the rabbi for his sustenance. This offering was called Challah. This name has evolved to identify the shape of a bread, although ingredients vary.

Wheat

    1   **cup warm water**
    4   **tablespoons honey**
    2   **tablespoons oil**
    3   **tablespoons kelp**
    2   **tablespoons yeast**
    3   **eggs**
    4   **cups whole wheat flour**
    1   **cup all-purpose flour**
        Cornmeal or sesame seeds
    1   **egg yolk, beaten**

Combine the first six ingredients in the Bosch bowl. Add the whole wheat flour, and begin kneading the dough. Gradually add the all-purpose flour until dough cleans the sides of the bowl. Knead dough 10 minutes. Lightly grease a baking sheet, and sprinkle with cornmeal or sesame seeds. Remove dough from bowl, and divide into three equal portions. Set aside one portion, and combine the other two. Divide the combined portion into three

equal parts. Roll each portion into a rope 14 to 16 inches long. Loosely braid the three ropes, and place on a baking sheet. Divide the remaining dough into three parts. Roll each into a rope 14 to 16 inches long. Loosely braid, and center on top of the first braid. Brush the entire loaf with the beaten egg yolk. Sprinkle with sesame seeds. Let rise until double. Bake in a 350° F. oven for 40 to 45 minutes. Serve while still warm. Makes 1 loaf.

Whole Wheat Challah

Wheat

    2   **tablespoons yeast**
    ½   **cup warm water**
    ¾   **cup milk**
    5   **tablespoons butter or margarine**
    2   **tablespoons honey**
    2   **teaspoons salt**
        Saffron (optional)
    2   **eggs**
    4   **cups whole wheat flour**
    1   **egg yolk**
    1   **tablespoon water**
        Poppy seeds

Sprinkle yeast over warm water in Bosch mixing bowl. In a small saucepan, combine milk, butter or margarine, honey, salt, and a dash of saffron. Heat to lukewarm. Pour into yeast mixture. Add eggs, and mix well. Mix in whole wheat flour. Knead 10 to 12 minutes. Cover, and let rise 1 hour. Divide dough into four equal portions. Roll three portions into 18-inch ropes. Loosely braid. Center on a large, greased baking sheet. Divide the remaining portion into three equal portions. Roll each one into an 18-inch rope. Loosely braid, and position on top of the first braid. Combine egg yolk and 1 tablespoon water. Brush both braids. Sprinkle with poppy seeds. Let rise until nearly double. Bake in a 350° F. oven for 30 to 35 minutes. Remove from baking sheet, and cool on wire rack. Makes 1 loaf.

Buttermilk-Cracked Wheat Bread
Wheat

     2 cups buttermilk
     2 tablespoons shortening
  ¼ cup honey
     1 tablespoon salt
  ¾-1 cup cracked wheat
     2 tablespoons yeast
  ½ cup warm water
  5-6 cups whole wheat flour
  ½ teaspoon baking soda

Combine buttermilk, shortening, honey, salt, and cracked wheat in a medium saucepan. Heat to lukewarm. Sprinkle yeast over warm water in Bosch mixing bowl. Allow to activate. When buttermilk mixture has cooled, add to the yeast mixture. Mix in whole wheat flour and baking soda. Knead 10 to 12 minutes. Divide dough into two portions. Shape into balls, and place in two well-greased 46-ounce juice cans. Let rise until 1 inch from the top of the can. Bake in a 350° F. oven for 35 to 40 minutes. Makes 2 loaves.

Buttermilk-Seed Bread

Substitute ½ cup sunflower seeds or sesame seeds for the cracked wheat.

Cottage Cheese-Raisin Bread
Wheat

     3 cups hot water
     2 cups raisins
     2 tablespoons yeast
     1 tablespoon salt
  1½ cups cottage cheese
     1 cup water
  8-9 cups whole wheat flour

Combine 3 cups hot water and raisins in Bosch blender. Blend just enough to coarsely chop. Pour into Bosch mixing bowl. Sprinkle yeast over raisins and water, and allow to activate. Add salt, cottage cheese, remaining 1 cup water, and flour. Mix well. Knead 10 to 12 minutes. Divide into three equal portions. Shape into loaves, and place in well-greased 8½ x 4½ x 2½-inch loaf pans. Let rise until double. Bake in a 350° F. oven for 45 minutes. Remove from pans, and let cool. Makes 3 loaves.

Yogurt Bread
Wheat

     4 cups yogurt
     1 cup water
  ¼ cup honey
  ⅓ cup oil
     3 tablespoons yeast
  ½ cup warm water
     1 teaspoon honey
     1 tablespoon salt
  10-12 cups whole wheat flour

Combine the yogurt, 1 cup water, ¼ cup honey, and oil in Bosch mixing bowl. In a small bowl, combine the yeast, ½ cup warm water, and 1 teaspoon honey. Allow yeast to activate. Add the yeast mixture, salt and flour to the yogurt mixture. Mix well. Knead 10 to 12 minutes. Divide into four loaves, and place in well-greased 46-ounce juice cans. Let rise until nearly double in size. Bake in a 350° F. oven for 40 minutes. Makes 4 loaves.

High-protein Yogurt Bread

To increase protein content by 20 to 25 percent, place ½ cup soybeans in Magic Mill III Plus™. Mill fine, and use to replace part of the whole wheat flour.

Dilly Bread
Wheat

  ½ cup warm water
     2 tablespoons yeast
     2 tablespoons honey or molasses
     1 cup cottage cheese, room temperature
     1 teaspoon salt
     2 tablespoons dill seed
     1 tablespoon dehydrated onion or
     2 tablespoons minced fresh onion
  ¼ teaspoon baking soda
     1 egg
  2-3 cups whole wheat flour

Combine water, yeast, and honey or molasses in Bosch mixing bowl. Allow yeast to activate. Add the remaining ingredients. Mix well. Knead 10 minutes. Cover, and let rise until double, approximately 1 hour. Shape into loaf, and place in a well-greased 8½ x 4½ x 2½-inch pan. Let rise until double. Bake in a 350° F. oven for 40 to 45 minutes. Makes 1 loaf.

Coolrise Honey-Lemon Bread
Wheat

>   2 cups whole wheat flour
>   2 tablespoons yeast
>   1 tablespoon salt
>   ¼ cup honey
>   3 tablespoons oil
>   1 tablespoon grated lemon peel
>   2¼ cups hot water
>   3½ cups whole wheat flour

Combine the 2 cups flour, yeast, and salt in Bosch
bowl. Add honey, oil, and lemon peel. Mix well.
Pour in hot water all at once. Add the remainder of
the flour, a little at a time, and knead for 12 minutes.
Divide dough into two equal portions. Form into
balls, and place in two well-greased 46-ounce cans.
Cover with plastic wrap, and refrigerate up to 24
hours. Remove from refrigerator, and let rise while
oven is heating. Bake in a 400° F. oven for 30
minutes. Makes 2 loaves.

Pumpkin-Oatmeal Bread
Wheat, oats

>   3 cups hot water
>   1 cup cooked, mashed pumpkin
>   1 cup cooked oatmeal
>   2 tablespoons honey
>   1 tablespoon salt
>   ¼ cup oil
>   2 tablespoons yeast
>   ½ cup warm water
>   8-9 cups whole wheat flour

Combine hot water, pumpkin, oatmeal, honey, salt,
and oil in Bosch bowl. Soften yeast in warm water in
a separate bowl, and add to ingredients in Bosch
bowl. Add flour, and knead mixture 10 minutes.
Shape into four loaves, and place in greased 7½ x
3½ x 2-inch bread pans. Let rise until double. Bake in
a 350° F. oven for 45 minutes. Remove from pans,
and cool on wire racks. Makes 4 loaves.

> NOTE: A crushed vitamin C tablet and 2 tablespoons of
> liquid lecithin give the bread a lighter texture. Two
> tablespoons lemon juice may be substituted for the
> vitamin C. One-half cup soybeans ground into soy flour
> may be substituted for lecithin.

Panattone Bread
Wheat

>   3 cups milk
>   2 tablespoons yeast
>   ½ cup water
>   3 eggs
>   2 cups citron
>   2 cups raisins
>   1 cup nuts (optional)
>   ½ teaspoon cardamom
>   2 teaspoons cinnamon
>   1 tablespoon salt
>   8-9 cups whole wheat flour

Scald milk, and allow to cool slightly. Combine yeast
and ½ cup water. Allow yeast to activate. Pour
cooled milk into Bosch bowl, and add eggs, citron,
raisins, nuts, spices, and salt. Add yeast. Add flour,
and knead for 10 minutes. Shape dough into two
large round loaves, and place on greased pizza
pans. Let rise until double. Bake in a 350° F. oven for
45 minutes. Cool on wire racks. Makes 2 loaves.

Cornmeal Bread
Wheat, corn

>   1 cup yellow cornmeal
>   2 cups cold water
>   2 cups hot water
>   ¾ cup honey
>   ½ cup butter or margarine
>   2 tablespoons salt
>   1½ cups warm water
>   3 tablespoons yeast
>   10-12 cups whole wheat flour
>   Cornmeal

In a 2-quart saucepan, combine cornmeal and cold
water. Add hot water, and cook over medium heat
until thickened. Remove from heat, and add honey,
butter or margarine, and salt. Cool to lukewarm.
Combine the warm water and yeast in Bosch mixing
bowl. Allow to activate. Add cornmeal mixture and
whole wheat flour. Mix well. Knead 10 to 12
minutes. Form into six loaves, and place in 7½ x 3½
x 2-inch loaf pans or 46-ounce juice cans that have
been well greased and lightly dusted with cornmeal.
Allow bread to double. Bake in a 375° F. oven for 15
minutes. Reduce heat to 325° and bake an
additional 25 minutes. Remove from pans and cool.
Makes 6 loaves.

Hot Toddy Bread
Wheat, oats, millet

- 1 cup whole oats
- 7 cups whole wheat
- 5 cups hot water
- ¼ cup honey
- ¼ cup molasses
- 1 vitamin C tablet, crushed
- ½ cup sunflower seeds
- ½ cup chopped walnuts
- ½ cup chopped cashews
- ½ cup millet
- 3 tablespoons yeast
- ⅓ cup dehydrated potato flakes
- ½ cup safflower oil
- 1½ tablespoons salt

Mill the oats and whole wheat in the Magic Mill III Plus™. In the Bosch mixing bowl, combine hot water, honey, molasses, vitamin C tablet, seeds, nuts, and millet. Add yeast, and allow to activate. Add the potato flakes, oil, and salt. Add oat flour and enough whole wheat flour to prevent dough from sticking to the sides of the bowl. Knead 10 minutes. Grease five 7½ x 3½ × 2-inch loaf pans. Shape dough into loaves and place in pans. Let rise until double. Bake in a 350° F. oven for 40 to 45 minutes. Remove from pans, and cool on cooling racks. Makes 5 loaves.

NOTE: For additional protein, half the oats may be replaced with soybeans. Coarsely grind with the oats.

Multigrain Bread
Wheat, mixed grains

- 1½ cups mixed grains*
- 8 cups whole wheat
- 5 cups hot water
- ½ cup molasses or honey
- 1 250 mg vitamin C tablet, crushed
- 3 tablespoons yeast
- ⅓ cup oil
- 2 tablespoons granulated lecithin
- 1½ tablespoons salt

Coarsely mill the mixed grain in the Magic Mill III Plus™. Remove from pan, and grind the wheat on the same setting. Combine water, molasses or honey, vitamin C, and yeast in Bosch mixing bowl. Let yeast activate. Add oil, lecithin, salt, mixed grain flour, and enough wheat flour to make a soft dough. Mix well. Knead 10 to 12 minutes, adding additional wheat flour as the kneading progresses until dough cleans the sides of the Bosch bowl. Divide dough into six equal portions, and shape into balls. Drop into well-greased 46-ounce juice cans. Let rise to within 1 inch of the top of the can. Bake in a 350° F. oven for 35 minutes. Makes 6 loaves.

*Barley, buckwheat, corn, millet, milo, oats, rice, rye, and wheat may be used. Soybeans, flax seed, and sunflower seeds are also good.

Ezekiel Bread

"Take thou also unto thee wheat, and barley, and beans, and lentiles, and millet, and fitches, and put them in one vessel, and make thee bread thereof." Ezekiel 4:9

Wheat, barley, rye, millet

- 7 cups wheat
- 1 cup barley
- ¼ cup pinto beans
- ¼ cup soybeans
- ¼ cup lentils
- 1 cup rye
- 5 cups hot water
- ½ cup butter or margarine
- ½ cup molasses or honey
- 3 tablespoons yeast
- 1½ tablespoons salt
- ⅓ cup millet
- ½ cup gluten flour (optional)

Combine the wheat, barley, pinto beans, soybeans, lentils, and rye, and mill in the Magic Mill III Plus. In the Bosch bowl, combine hot water, butter or margarine, molasses or honey, yeast, and salt. Add multigrain flour, millet, and gluten flour until dough pulls away from the sides of the bowl. Knead 10 minutes. Shape into four round loaves, and place on two well-greased baking sheets. Let rise until double. Bake in a 350° F. oven for 35 minutes. Makes 4 loaves.

Pumpernickel Bread
Wheat, rye, corn

>   4   tablespoons yeast
>   3 ½   cups warm water
>   ½   cup molasses or honey
>   1   tablespoon oil
>   2   tablespoons salt
>   2   cups mashed potatoes
>   ¾   cup cornmeal
>   2   teaspoons caraway seeds (optional)
>   ½   cup sunflower seeds (optional)
>   2   tablespoons carob powder
>   3   cups rye flour
> 9-10   cups whole wheat flour

Sprinkle yeast over water in Bosch mixing bowl. Allow to activate. Add the remaining ingredients, and mix well. Knead 10 to 12 minutes. For lighter loaves, allow dough to rise until double. However, bread may be shaped immediately. Divide dough into four equal portions, and place in four well-greased 8½ x 4½ x 2½-inch loaf pans. (Dough may also be shaped into free-form loaves and placed on a baking sheet that has been greased and lightly dusted with cornmeal.) Allow to double. Bake in a 350° F. oven for 50 minutes. Occasionally brush with water as it bakes for a chewy crust. Makes 4 loaves.

> NOTE: All-purpose flour may be used for half the whole wheat flour. If using instant mashed potatoes, combine 1½ cups water, ½ cup milk, ½ teaspoon salt, and ½ cup instant mashed potato. Whip with electric mixer until fluffy, and then add to bread.

Rye Bread
Rye

>   2   cups Sourdough Starter (page 22)
>   3   cups warm water
>   2   tablespoons yeast
>   1   tablespoon salt
>   ⅓   cup molasses
>   ⅓   cup oil
>   6-8   cups rye flour
>   Cornmeal

Combine Sourdough Starter, water, and yeast in Bosch mixing bowl. Allow yeast to activate. Add the remaining ingredients, and mix well. Knead 10 to 12 minutes. Do not add too much flour; dough should remain sticky and pliable. When kneaded, shape into two round, free-form loaves. Place on a lightly greased baking sheet that has been sprinkled with cornmeal. Let rise for at least 90 minutes. Bake in a 400° F. oven for 45 minutes. Makes 2 loaves.

Rye-Wheat Bread
Rye, wheat

>   3   cups milk
>   2   tablespoons yeast
>   4   tablespoons honey
>   3   tablespoons oil
>   1   tablespoon salt
>   4   cups rye flour
>   4   cups whole wheat flour

Scald milk and let cool to lukewarm. Pour into Bosch mixing bowl. Sprinkle yeast over milk, and let soften. Add honey, oil, and salt. Stir in 3 cups rye flour and 3 cups whole wheat flour. Knead 12 minutes, adding the remaining flour as needed. Cover, and let dough rest 2 hours. Punch down, and then divide in half. Shape into two round loaves or two long loaves. Place on a large, well-greased baking sheet, cover, and let rise until nearly double. Bake in a 375° F. oven for 40 to 50 minutes. Bread should sound hollow when tapped. Remove from baking sheet, and cool on wire racks. Makes 2 loaves.

> NOTE: Warm water may be used in place of the milk.

Cottage Rye Bread

Thinly slice this dense, moist bread and serve with cheese.

Rye

           2 **cups warm water**
           3 **tablespoons yeast**
          ⅓ **cup molasses**
        1¼ **cups cottage cheese**
           1 **cup dry powdered milk**
           1 **200 mg vitamin C tablet, crushed (optional)**
           2 **tablespoons granulated lecithin (optional)**
      9-10 **cups rye flour**
        4½ **teaspoons salt**
          ¼ **cup oil**
           3 **tablespoons caraway seeds (optional)**
           1 **egg white, beaten**
              Sesame seeds

Combine water, yeast, and molasses in Bosch mixing bowl. Allow yeast to soften. Add cottage cheese, dry powdered milk, crushed vitamin C tablet, lecithin, and 4 cups rye flour. Mix together well. Let rise 1 hour. Add salt, oil, caraway seeds, and remaining flour. Knead 10 to 12 minutes. Do not add more flour than necessary to knead. Dough should be sticky and pliable. Shape into three round loaves. Place on well-greased baking sheets. Brush with egg white, and sprinkle with sesame seeds. Let rise at least 1¼ hours at room temperature. Bake in a 350° F. oven for 45 minutes. Makes 3 loaves.

Finnish Sour Rye Bread

Wheat, rye

STARTER:
        1½ **cups buttermilk or water**
           1 **cup rye flour**
DOUGH:
          ¼ **cup warm water**
           2 **tablespoons yeast**
           2 **teaspoons salt**
        1½ **cups buttermilk or water**
        2½ **cups rye flour**
   3½-4 **cups whole wheat flour**
              Cornmeal
           1 **egg white, beaten**
              Sesame seeds

To prepare starter, combine buttermilk or water and 1 cup rye flour in a quart jar. Cover and allow to stand at room temperature for 4 days. Stir once or twice daily.

To prepare bread, pour warm water into Bosch mixing bowl. Sprinkle yeast over water, and allow to activate. Add starter. Stir in salt, buttermilk or water, rye flour, and whole wheat flour. Knead 10 to 12 minutes. Cover and let rise 1½ hours. Brush baking sheets with shortening, and sprinkle with cornmeal. Divide dough into two equal portions. Shape into long French loaves, and place on baking sheets. Let rise 15 to 20 minutes. Brush lightly with beaten egg white, and sprinkle with sesame seeds. Slash top diagonally three or four times. Let rise until double. Place in an unheated oven, set temperature at 400° F., and turn on oven. Bake 15 minutes, then reduce heat to 350° F. and bake an additional 25 to 30 minutes. Remove from baking sheets, and cool on cooling rack. Makes 2 loaves.

> NOTE: All-purpose flour may be used instead of or in combination with the whole wheat flour. A tablespoon of caraway seeds may be added with the buttermilk or water for a rich caraway flavor.

Black Russian Rye Bread

A rich and chewy bread. Thinly slice, and enjoy with butter or cream cheese.

Wheat, rye

2 tablespoons yeast
½ cup warm water
2 cups water
¼ cup vinegar
½ cup molasses
4½ tablespoons carob powder
¼ cup butter or margarine
1 tablespoon salt
2 teaspoons Postum powder
2 tablespoons dehydrated onion
4 tablespoons crushed caraway seed
½ teaspoon crushed fennel seed
4 cups rye flour
4-5 cups whole wheat flour
Cornmeal
½ cup cold water
1 teaspoon cornstarch

In Bosch mixing bowl, soften yeast in ½ cup warm water. In a small saucepan, combine 2 cups water, vinegar, molasses, carob powder, butter or margarine, salt, Postum, dehydrated onion, caraway seed, and fennel seed. Heat to lukewarm. Add to yeast mixture. Add rye flour, and stir. Add most of the whole wheat flour. Knead 10 to 12 minutes, adding flour as needed. Lightly grease a baking sheet and sprinkle with cornmeal. Divide dough into two portions, and form into balls. Place on each end of the baking sheet. Cover with a towel, and let rise until double. (Do not put free-formed loaves in a warmed oven to rise.) Bake in a 350° F. oven for 45 to 50 minutes. While bread is baking, combine ½ cup cold water and cornstarch in a small saucepan. Cook until thickened. Remove bread from oven, brush with cornstarch mixture, and return to oven for an additional 2 to 3 minutes to set the glaze. Remove from baking sheet, and place loaves on cooling rack to cool. Makes 2 loaves.

NOTE: For a lighter bread, decrease rye flour and increase wheat flour, or use 3 cups all-purpose flour and 2 cups whole wheat flour instead of the 4 to 5 cups whole wheat flour.

Dark Rye Bread

Rye, wheat

2½ cups milk
2 tablespoons yeast
½ cup warm water
4 cups rye flour
4 cups whole wheat flour
3 tablespoons molasses
3 tablespoons oil
1 tablespoon salt
Cornmeal

Scald milk, and cool to lukewarm. In a small bowl, add yeast to warm water, and allow to activate. Combine flours in Bosch mixing bowl. Add molasses, oil, and salt. Add the scalded milk and yeast mixture. Blend until well mixed. Cover dough with a towel, and let proof for 15 to 20 minutes. Knead for 12 minutes. Add additional flour if needed. Shape into two round loaves. Place on a greased baking sheet that has been lightly sprinkled with cornmeal. Cover with a towel, and let rise 30 minutes or until dough has risen about one-third. (Bread will not raise as high as 100 percent whole wheat bread because of the rye content.) Bake in a 350° F. oven for 50 to 60 minutes. Makes 2 loaves.

NOTE: Water may be used in place of the milk.

eam cheese and chives make a delicious and nutritious sandwich on Black Russian Rye Bread.

Butter Rolls
Wheat

- **2 cups milk**
- **2 tablespoons honey**
- **2 tablespoons yeast**
- **2 eggs, beaten**
- **1 teaspoon salt**
- **5-6 cups whole wheat flour**
- **½ cup butter, softened**

Scald milk, and cool to lukewarm. Pour into Bosch bowl, and add honey and yeast. Let yeast activate. Add eggs, salt, and flour. Knead for 10 to 12 minutes. Let rise 1 hour. Roll out into a large rectangle. Spread with one-third of the butter, fold over, and roll out again. Repeat until all butter is used. Roll out to ½-inch thickness and cut with a biscuit cutter. Place on greased baking sheets, and let rise for 1 to 2 hours. Bake in a 375° F. oven for 20 minutes. Makes 2 dozen.

Cardamom Honey Rolls

Follow above recipe, increasing honey to 4 tablespoons and adding ½ teaspoon cardamom.

NOTE: Two cups all-purpose flour may be substituted for 2 cups whole wheat flour.

Carmene's Fantastic Rolls
Wheat

- **5 cups hot water**
- **1 cup honey**
- **1 cup dry powdered milk**
- **4 tablespoons yeast**
- **4 eggs**
- **12-13 cups whole wheat flour**
- **4 teaspoons salt**
- **1 cup oil**
- **Melted butter**

Combine hot water, honey, powdered milk, and yeast in Bosch bowl. Allow yeast to activate. Add eggs and 7 cups flour. Stir until thoroughly mixed; dough will resemble cake batter. Let rest until bubbly, about 30 minutes. Add salt, oil, and remaining flour. Knead for 10 minutes. Pour out onto a lightly greased surface. Grease baking sheets. Pinch off 2-inch round portions, and roll out to an 8-inch rope. Tie rope in a single knot. Place in rows on

baking sheets, cover, and let rise until double. Bake in a 350° F. oven for 25 minutes or until lightly browned. Brush with melted butter, and remove to a cooling rack. Makes 4 dozen.

NOTE: When kneading this recipe by hand, knead on a floured surface for 10 minutes until dough is soft and pliable. Shape into a ball, oil surface with 2 tablespoons oil, cover, and let rise until double. Punch down, and let rise again. Shape as above, or select an alternate shape.

Fifty-fifty Rolls

Substitute all-purpose flour for half of the whole wheat flour.

Multigrain Rolls

Substitute a single-grain flour, such as corn, millet, barley, or rye, or a multigrain flour for 2 cups of the whole wheat flour.

Bubble Loaf

Prepare batter for Carmene's Fantastic Rolls as directed. Combine ⅓ cup packed brown sugar and 1 teaspoon cinnamon in a small bowl. Using half of the roll dough, make a long rope 1 inch in diameter. Cut into 1-inch pieces. Dip each piece in melted butter or margarine, and roll in sugar and cinnamon mixture. Place pieces in a greased 10-inch tube pan. Pieces should be just touching. Sprinkle with nuts. Place maraschino cherries and raisins in crevasses. Cover, and let rise until double. Bake in a 350° F. oven for 35 minutes. Remove from oven and invert immediately. Break apart to serve.

Whole Wheat Danish Rolls
Wheat

    3 tablespoons yeast
1½ cups warm water
    ½ cup cup packed brown sugar
    ¼ cup honey
    ¼ teaspoon mace
    ¼ teaspoon nutmeg
    ½ teaspoon lemon extract
    ½ cup butter
    3 eggs
    5 cups whole wheat flour
    ½ cup butter
       Brown Sugar Topping (below)

Combine yeast and water, and set aside. In the Bosch bowl, cream together brown sugar, honey, mace, nutmeg, lemon extract and ½ cup butter. Add eggs, and beat well. Scrape down from sides of bowl. Add flour and yeast. Mix for 5 to 7 minutes, and turn out onto a lightly floured sheet. Cover with a towel, and refrigerate for 1 hour. On a lightly floured surface, roll dough out to a rectangle about ½ inch in thickness. Spread generously with remaining ½ cup butter. Fold dough into thirds, and roll out again. Repeat folding and rolling one more time. Replace dough on the lightly floured sheet, cover, and chill for an additional hour. Shape rolls as desired, and let rise until double. Bake in a 400° F. oven for 8 minutes. Spread with Brown Sugar Topping while still warm. Makes 2 dozen.

Brown Sugar Topping

    ⅓ cup packed brown sugar
    1 tablespoon margarine
    1 tablespoon water
    1 tablespoon honey

Combine ingredients in a small saucepan, and bring to a boil. Cool slightly before using.

Twelve-Hour Butterhorns
Wheat

    1 cup milk
    ½ cup warm water
    1 tablespoon packed brown sugar
    4 tablespoons yeast
    6 eggs
    1 cup butter or margarine
    1 cup honey
8-10 cups whole wheat flour
    ¾ tablespoon salt
    1 teaspoon cardamom
       Melted butter
       Brown sugar
       Cinnamon
       Confectioners' Icing (below)

Scald milk, and then cool to lukewarm. In a separate bowl, combine water, brown sugar, and yeast. In Bosch bowl equipped with wire whips, blend together eggs, butter or margarine, and honey. Insert dough hook. Add 8 cups whole wheat flour, salt, cardamom, milk, and yeast. Knead for 12 minutes. Add flour as needed to make a soft but not too sticky dough. Lightly oil hands and the inside of a large bowl. Transfer dough, and turn to coat dough with oil. Cover, and let rise 6 hours. Punch down. Divide dough in half, and roll out each half to a large rectangle ⅜-inch in thickness. Brush with melted butter, and generously sprinkle with brown sugar and cinnamon. Roll up , and cut into ½-inch pieces. Place 1 inch apart on well-greased baking sheets, and let rise an additional 6 hours. Bake in a 350° F. oven for 20 minutes. Frost with Confectioners' Icing. Makes 2 dozen.

Confectioners' Icing

1-2 tablespoons light cream
    2 cups powdered sugar
       Salt
    1 teaspoon vanilla or almond flavoring

Add light cream to powdered sugar to achieve spreading consistency. Add a dash of salt and flavoring. Blend until smooth.

Danish Pastry Wreath

A light and fluffy pastry with a texture in a realm all by itself.

Wheat

PASTRY:
- 1½ **cups butter, softened**
- ¼ **cup whole wheat flour**
- ¾ **cup warm milk**
- ⅓ **cup honey**
- 1 **teaspoon salt**
- ½ **cup warm water**
- 2 **tablespoons yeast**
- 2 **eggs**
- 3-3¾ **cups whole wheat flour**

FILLING:
- ½ **cup butter, melted**
- 1 **egg**
- 1 **8-ounce can almond paste**
- ¾ **cup fine dry whole wheat bread crumbs**
- ½ **teaspoon almond extract**

Beat butter and ¼ cup flour until smooth. Fasten a sheet of waxed paper to a smooth surface with a little water. Spread butter/flour mixture on waxed paper to form an 8 x 12-inch rectangle. Transfer waxed paper to a cookie sheet and refrigerate. Warm the milk in a small saucepan. Add honey and salt. Pour warm water into Bosch bowl. Add yeast, and let activate. Add milk mixture, eggs, and enough flour to make a stiff dough. Knead 10 to 12 minutes. Remove from Bosch bowl, shape into a ball, oil lightly, and place in a large bowl. Cover with a towel, and refrigerate for 30 minutes. Turn out onto a lightly floured surface, and roll out to a 12 x 16-inch rectangle. Place the butter/flour mixture on half the dough. Fold the other half of the dough over the top. Pinch to seal edges. Roll dough out to an 8 x 16-inch rectangle. Fold into thirds, seal edges, and chill for 1 hour. Roll again to an 8 x 16-inch rectangle, fold into thirds and seal edges. Chill 30 minutes more. Repeat rolling, folding, and sealing procedure one more time. Wrap in foil, and chill 3 hours or overnight.

Using half the dough (keep the other half refrigerated), roll out the dough into an 8 x 22-inch rectangle. Cut into thirds lengthwise to create three long strips of dough. Combine filling ingredients, and spread half the filling lengthwise down the center of each strip. Roll each third into a long rope, and seal the edges. Loosely braid the three ropes. Place on a well-greased cookie sheet, and form into

a wreath. Seal ends. Prepare second wreath in same manner. Allow to rise in a warm place until double, approximately 1 hour. Bake in a 375° F. oven for 30 minutes or until golden brown. Makes 2 wreaths.

NOTE: A variety of fillings may be used instead of the almond paste, such as cinnamon and sugar, ground dates and raisins moistened with applesauce, mincemeat, chopped nuts, or any combination.

Cinnamon Rolls

Prepare dough as directed. After final chilling, roll out into an 8 x 22-inch strip, and spread with brown sugar, cinnamon, raisins, or selected filling. Roll up, and cut into ½-inch slices. Place on a greased cookie sheet, let double in size, and bake in a 375° F. oven for 20 minutes or until golden brown. Glaze with powdered sugar icing, if desired.

Brown Sugar Filling

In a small bowl combine ½ cup butter or margarine, 1 cup packed brown sugar, 2 teaspoons cinnamon, ⅔ cup chopped nuts or sunflower seeds, and ½ cup raisins. Spread mixture generously over dough in place of the almond filling. Braid and bake as directed.

Greek Wedding Ring
Wheat

2 cups whole wheat flour
2 cups all-purpose flour
2 tablespoons yeast
1½ cups milk
2 tablespoons grated lemon rind
2 tablespoons grated orange rind
½ cup butter or margarine
½ teaspoon anise seed
⅓ cup honey
1½ teaspoons salt
3 eggs, beaten
1 egg, separated
1 tablespoon milk
Melted butter or margarine

Combine the flours and the yeast in the Bosch bowl. Mix the 1½ cups milk, lemon and orange rind, butter or margarine, anise seed, honey, and salt in a small saucepan. Heat to 115° (lukewarm). Add to the flour and yeast in the Bosch bowl. Add the 3 eggs. Knead for 10 minutes. Turn dough out onto a lightly greased surface. Pinch off about 1 cup dough, and set aside. Roll remaining dough into a 12 x 18-inch rectangle. Roll up dough, beginning at the 18-inch edge. Form into a circle. Position on a greased pizza pan or large baking sheet, pressing the two ends together. Slightly beat the egg white, and brush the ring. With the rolling pin, roll out the reserved 1 cup dough to ¼-inch thickness. Using kitchen shears, cut out diamonds, hearts, flowers, strips for dainty braids, or other decorations. Attractively position cutouts on the dough ring, and gently push into place so they will not come off as the bread raises. Brush entire loaf with the remaining egg yolk mixed with 1 tablespoon milk. Let rise 1 hour or until double. Bake in a 350° F. oven for 45 minutes. Remove from pan, and brush with melted butter or margarine. Serves 10 to 12.

Spudnuts
Wheat

2 tablespoons yeast
½ cup warm water
1 cup hot mashed potatoes
4 tablespoons butter or margarine
1½ cups warm milk
4 tablespoons honey
2 eggs
2 teaspoons salt
¾ teaspoon nutmeg
¾ teaspoon cinnamon
3½ cups whole wheat flour
3½ cups all-purpose flour
Deep-fat cooking oil
Glaze (below)

In a small bowl, combine yeast and warm water. Let activate. Combine mashed potatoes, butter or margarine, milk, honey, and eggs in Bosch bowl. Stir in yeast. Add salt, nutmeg, cinnamon, and 3 cups of each flour. Knead 12 minutes. Add remaining flour until dough cleans the sides of the bowl. Cover, and let rise 1 hour. Turn out dough onto a lightly oiled surface, and roll out to just under ½-inch thickness. Cut with a doughnut cutter. (For a larger doughnut, open both ends of a tuna can, and use to cut the outer circle. Use a vanilla bottle lid to cut the hole.) Place doughnuts on a muslin dish towel which has been lightly dusted with flour. Let rise 30 minutes. Gently lift off doughnuts, and lower into hot 350° F. cooking oil. Fry until brown, and then turn. Drain on paper toweling. Dip hot doughnuts into Glaze, and drain. Makes 3 dozen.

Glaze

1 pound powdered sugar
4 tablespoons butter or margarine
1 teaspoon vanilla
Hot water

Pour powdered sugar into a small bowl. Beat in butter or margarine and vanilla. Add hot water until glaze is thin.

Maple Bars
Wheat

3 tablespoons yeast
¼ cup warm water
½ cup margarine
½ cup sugar or honey
3 eggs
1 teaspoon salt
½ teaspoon vanilla
½ teaspoon lemon flavoring
2 cups milk or water
4½ cups whole wheat flour
3 cups all-purpose flour
Deep-fat cooking oil
Maple Frosting (below)

In Bosch bowl, soften yeast in ¼ cup water. Add the margarine, sugar or honey, eggs, salt, vanilla, lemon flavoring, milk or water, and flours. Knead 10 minutes. Cover, and let rise 1 hour. Stir down, and turn out onto a lightly oiled surface. Roll out to ¼-inch thickness, and cut into oblong shapes, approximately 3 inches long. Deep-fat fry in 360° F. cooking oil until golden brown. Drain on paper toweling. While still warm, glaze with Maple Frosting. Makes about 4 dozen.

Maple Frosting

4 cups powdered sugar
3 tablespoons butter or margarine, softened
3-4 tablespoons hot water
½-1 tablespoon maple flavoring

Combine powdered sugar and butter or margarine in a small bowl. Add water to achieve spreading consistency. Add maple flavoring to taste.

Armenian Thin Bread
Wheat

2 cups warm water
2 tablespoons yeast
2 tablespoons honey
1 tablespoon salt
¼ cup butter or margarine, melted
5 cups whole wheat flour
1 egg
¼ cup water
Sesame seeds

Sprinkle yeast over water in the Bosch bowl, and allow to activate. Add the honey, salt, butter or margarine, and flour, and knead for 10 to 12 minutes. Shape dough into a ball, oil the surface, and place in a bowl. Cover with a towel, and let rise until double. Punch down, and divide into twelve equal portions. On a lightly floured board, roll each piece of dough to a paper-thin consistency. Place on baking sheets. Combine egg and water, and brush lightly over dough. Sprinkle generously with sesame seeds. Prick with a fork. Let rise 45 minutes. Place oven racks at the lowest and highest levels, and set oven temperature at 400° F. When oven is hot, place one baking sheet on each oven rack. Bake for 4 minutes, and then switch the location of the two sheets. Bake an additional 4 minutes. Small bubbles will form across the top of the bread. Bread should be lightly browned. Remove from baking sheets to cool. Makes 12.

NOTE: If the number of baking sheets is limited, place extra disks of dough on a muslin dishtowel while others are baking.

Rye Armenian Thin Bread

Substitute 2½ cups rye flour for 2½ cups of the whole wheat flour. Add ¾ teaspoon caraway seeds and ½ teaspoon anise seeds. Mix as directed.

White Armenian Thin Bread

Substitute all-purpose flour for the whole wheat flour. Bread will resemble the consistency of a soda cracker, except chewier.

Armenian Roll Up

Generously spray baked Armenian Thin Bread with water, and allow to soften. Spread with yogurt, top with desired meat filling, and roll up.

Pita Bread
Wheat, rye, millet

6 **cups whole wheat flour**
2 **teaspoons salt**
½ **cup warm water**
1 **teaspoon honey or molasses**
2 **tablespoons yeast**
1½-2 **cups warm water**
2 **tablespoons oil**

Measure flour into Bosch bowl. Mix in salt. In one side of the flour, make a slight depression. Pour the ½ cup warm water, honey or molasses, and yeast into this well. Let sit for 5 minutes or until yeast bubbles. Begin stirring dough, adding just enough of the remaining water to moisten nearly all of the flour. Enough dry flour should be left for kneading the bread. Knead 5 minutes. Shape into a ball, oil with 2 tablespoons oil, place in a bowl, and cover with a towel. Let rise 1 hour. Transfer dough onto a lightly floured surface, and divide into sixteen equal pieces. Shape into balls, cover, and let rest 10 minutes. Roll the dough into circles about 6 inches in diameter and ¼ inch in thickness. Place on ungreased baking sheets, cover, and let rise 30 minutes. Place the oven rack in its highest position, and preheat oven to 500° F. Bake for 8 to 10 minutes. Pita Bread will puff up and form a pocket. If it does not open, the dough was not rolled thinly enough. Bread should be lightly browned. Cool on a cooling rack. Makes 16.

NOTE: Place Pita Bread in a plastic bag while still warm to keep it soft and pliable.

Millet Pita

Substitute 3 cups all-purpose flour for 3 cups whole wheat flour. Add 1½ cups each of whole wheat and millet flour.

Caraway Rye Pita

Use 3 cups all-purpose flour, 1½ cups whole wheat flour, and 1½ cups rye flour. Add 2 teaspoons caraway seeds with the rye flour.

Bagels
Wheat

2 **cups warm water**
2 **tablespoons honey**
2 **tablespoons yeast**
3 **teaspoons salt**
5 **cups whole wheat flour**
1 **tablespoon honey**
3 **quarts water**
  Cornmeal
1 **egg yolk, beaten**
1 **tablespoon water**
  Sesame seeds (optional)

Combine 2 cups warm water, honey, and yeast in Bosch bowl. Let yeast activate. Add salt and flour, and knead 10 minutes. Cover, and let rise 45 minutes. Remove from bowl, and divide into twelve equal portions. Shape each into a smooth ball. Poke fingers through center and shape into a doughnut with a large hole. Place on a lightly floured surface. Cover, and let rise 30 minutes. In a large kettle, bring honey and 3 quarts water to a gentle boil. Grease a baking sheet, and lightly sprinkle with cornmeal. Gently lift bagels into boiling water. Several may be boiled at one time. Simmer 5 minutes, turning often. Drain on paper toweling, and then transfer to baking sheets. Brush with egg wash prepared with beaten egg yolk and 1 tablespoon water. Sprinkle with sesame seeds, if desired. Bake in a 400° F. oven for 35 to 40 minutes. Makes 1 dozen.

NOTE: For a lighter bagel, replace half the whole wheat flour with white.

Rye Bagels

Use 4 cups whole wheat flour and 1 cup rye flour. Substitute molasses for the honey, and add 1 tablespoon caraway seeds.

Lemon Loaf (page 44) takes its place beside Eight-grain Muffins (page 45), Texas Corn Bread (page 44), and Baking Powder Biscuits (page 4

Quick Breads

Quick Breads

The term **quick breads** refers to any type of bread product which does not use yeast as a leavening agent. The recipes in this section begin with loaf breads and proceed through muffins, biscuits, and crackers. Included next are unleavened deep-fat fried breads, followed by griddle breads which include crepes, pancakes, and waffles.

Thin Breads

Every culture has some type of unleavened bread. In many nations, where wheat is not the dominant grain, a flat cake is made of the native grain. Knockbrod, sopapilla, tortillas, crepes, and chapati are some examples. They contain little, if any, leavening agents.

Making sandwiches out of these breads would be difficult, but they are rich and good. They taste great alongside sandwich makings or wrapped around them. Start with any combination of cooked, sliced meats. Add chopped onions, lettuce, sprouts, shredded cheese or sour cream. Try tuna fish salad. Remember the Mexican influence and fill with thick chili or the makings for tacos.

A combination of avocadoes, tomatoes, and watercress makes a good complement to thin breads. Even such dishes as refried beans, falafel or sauerkraut taste good. The old standby, peanut butter and jelly, is a great filling.

Crepes

Crepes are the favorite unleavened bread of the French. They are sold by vendors on the streets and on the ski slopes. The thin bread can be filled with exotic combinations or simply sprinkled with sugar and eaten as a finger food.

Crepes can be made from variety grains to obtain unique flavors. The best crepes are those that are 100 percent whole wheat or approximately half and half with another grain. However, buckwheat and rye both make excellent crepes by themselves.

Crepes mixed in a blender may be used immediately. Crepes mixed by hand should set for 2 to 3 hours to allow the flour and liquid to mix thoroughly. For more tender crepes, refrigerate and rest the batter overnight. Batter may be refrigerated up to a week. Stir before using as the contents will separate.

Choose the type of crepe pan that you are the most comfortable with. Styles range from electric pans that are dipped into the batter to well-seasoned cast-iron pans. The pan should be heated before adding batter so that the batter will cook quickly. Crepes are only cooked on one side. When rolling the crepe, this lightly browned side should face out.

After cooking crepes, fill and roll. The most common method is to put the filling along one edge and roll. Crepe filling may also be placed in the center of the crepe. Fold in the two outsides. Roll crepe and serve with folded side down. Another method is to place the filling in the lower right-hand corner near the center. Fold crepe in half over the filling and then in half again, forming a pie-shaped wedge.

Cooked, unfilled crepes may be frozen for future use. Stack them and enclose in a plastic bag from which all the air has been removed. Allow crepes to defrost at room temperature.

The variety of crepe fillings is limited only by your imagination. Here are a few suggestions you might like to try:

Left-over casseroles are enhanced by putting 1 to 2 tablespoons of casserole in a crepe. Heat through, and serve with gravy, cream sauce, or cream soup over the top. Cheese sauce, made by combining a white sauce with your favorite shredded cheese, is also excellent.

Custard pudding inside a crepe is delicious when served with chocolate sauce and whipped cream.

Canned pie filling makes a quick and tasty filling. Spoon two tablespoons of your favorite pie filling, such as cherry, blueberry, or apple, inside the crepe. Roll up, and crown with a dollop of whipped cream.

Assorted fruits, canned peaches, pears, or bananas, can be rolled in a crepe and heated. Thicken fruit juice to make a sauce and add ice cream on top.

For an **apple stack** of crepes, sauté 6 cups of sliced apples in 4 tablespoons of butter, stirring constantly. Add ¼ cup water, cover, and steam for 5 minutes. Add ¾ cup brown sugar and cinnamon to taste. Using alternate layers of crepes and fried apples, stack until apples or crepes run out. Drizzle a powdered sugar icing over all. Cut into wedges, and serve with ice cream.

Chicken-wheat crepes may be prepared by combining 2 cups diced cooked chicken, 1 cup cooked whole kernel wheat, 1 to 1½ cans of cream of chicken soup, and 1½ cups chicken gravy. Add soy sauce to taste. Roll filling in crepes and top with a sauce of cream of chicken soup diluted with a little milk.

South of the border crepes are made by filling a crepe with a barbecue beef mixture and heating. Serve topped with sour cream, chopped onion, and shredded cheese.

Deli crepes are simple and delicious. Fill crepes with thinly sliced cooked chicken, ham, and Swiss cheese. Put under the broiler to warm.

For **omelet** crepes, fill crepes with scrambled eggs,

cooked bacon, sausage, or ham. Top with chili sauce.

Spread **peanut butter and jelly** on a crepe. Roll up and enjoy as a finger food.

Vegetarian crepes may contain fried mushrooms and bean sprouts. Top with slightly diluted cream of mushroom soup. Sprinkle with chopped onion and chopped nuts.

Pilafs are excellent when used as a crepe filling. Top with a complementary sauce.

Pancakes and Waffles

Pancakes and waffles are not often thought of as unleavened breads, but they are. These two favorite breakfast foods can also be served as a fancy dessert or a light evening meal. Batter for pancakes and waffles may be used interchangeably. Thin pancake batter for waffles. Add more flour to waffle batter for pancakes.

Try some of these toppings on pancakes or waffles:

Peach Sauce

In a heavy saucepan, mash 2½ cups ripe or canned peaches. Add ¼ teaspoon salt and 1 tablespoon cornstarch. Cook until clear and thick, stirring constantly. Add 1 tablespoon butter and ¼ teaspoon nutmeg. Sweeten with a little sugar or honey, if desired.

Orange Honey

Combine 1 cup honey, 1 cup orange juice, and ⅓ cup butter. Heat and serve.

Rye-Raisin Syrup

Stir ½ cup whipping cream or evaporated milk with 1 tablespoon rye flour. Add 1½ cups water, ½ cup honey, ½ cup dark corn syrup, ¼ cup butter, ¼ teaspoon cinnamon, and 1 cup raisins. Simmer, stirring constantly, until mixture is thick and clear.

Fruit Butter

Combine 1½ cups chopped dried fruit, ¾ cup orange juice, 1 tablespoon honey, ¼ teaspoon cinnamon, and a dash of cloves. Simmer for 10 minutes. Blend in a blender.

Lemon Loaf
Wheat

        ½ cup butter or margarine
        1 cup sugar
        2 eggs
        2 teaspoons lemon rind
    1 ½ cups whole wheat flour
        1 teaspoon baking powder
        ¼ teaspoon salt
        ½ cup milk
        ¼ cup sugar
        1 lemon, juiced

Cream butter or margarine and sugar in Bosch bowl. Blend in eggs and lemon rind. Combine dry ingredients, and alternately add to egg mixture with milk, stirring after each addition. Pour into a well-greased 8½ x 4½-inch pan, and bake in a 350° F. oven for 60 minutes or until a toothpick inserted in the center comes out clean. Remove from pan, and while still warm, puncture top of loaf with a fork. Combine ¼ cup sugar and lemon juice, and pour slowly over loaf. Set on rack to cool. Wrap in foil for 2 days before serving. Makes 1 loaf.

Carob-Zucchini Bread
Wheat, barley

        6 tablespoons butter or margarine, softened
        ½ cup sugar
        1 egg
        ¼ cup milk
        1 teaspoon vanilla
        1 teaspoon grated orange rind
        1 cup grated zucchini
        1 cup whole wheat flour
        ¼ cup barley flour
        ¼ cup carob powder
        ¼ teaspoon baking soda
    1¾ teaspoons baking powder
        ½ teaspoon salt
        ½ teaspoon cinnamon

Cream together butter or margarine and sugar in Bosch bowl. Add egg, milk, and vanilla, and stir until well blended. Add orange rind and zucchini. Combine dry ingredients in a separate bowl, and then add to zucchini batter. Pour into a well-greased 8½ x 4½-inch loaf pan. Bake in a 350° F. oven for 30 minutes. Makes 1 loaf.

Barley Bread
Barley

    1½ cups barley flour
        ½ teaspoon salt
        4 teaspoons baking powder
    1½ tablespoons oil
        1 egg
        ½ cup milk
        2 tablespoons honey

Combine dry ingredients in a small mixing bowl. Blend oil, eggs, milk, and honey in Bosch blender. Add to dry ingredients, and stir only until mixed. Pour into a greased 8 x 8-inch pan. Bake in a 350° F. oven for 20 minutes. Cut into squares, and serve hot. Serves 4 to 6.

Barley Loaf

Prepare Barley Bread as directed. Bake in a greased 8½ x 4½ x 2½-inch loaf pan for 30 to 35 minutes.

Texas Corn Bread
Corn

        2 eggs
        2 cups buttermilk
        3 tablespoons oil
    2½ cups cornmeal
    1½ teaspoons salt
        1 tablespoon baking powder
        ½ tablespoon baking soda

Beat eggs in the Bosch bowl until light. Stir in buttermilk and oil. Combine dry ingredients in a separate bowl. Mix into buttermilk mixture until batter is smooth. Pour into a greased 9 x 9-inch pan. Bake in a 425° F. oven for 25 minutes. Serves 4 to 6.

Sourdough Rice Bread

Rice

- 1½ cups rice flour
- ¾ teaspoon baking soda
- ½ teaspoon salt
- 1 cup Sourdough Starter (page 22)
- 1 13-ounce can evaporated milk
- 2 eggs
- 2 tablespoons honey or molasses
- 4 tablespoons melted butter or margarine

Combine dry ingredients in a small bowl. In Bosch bowl, combine starter, evaporated milk, eggs, honey or molasses, and melted butter or margarine. Add dry ingredients to moist ingredients, and stir only enough to combine. Pour into a well-greased, cast-iron frying pan or a 9 x 13-inch baking dish. Bake in a 425° F. oven for 25 minutes. Serves 6 to 8.

Applesauce Muffins

Wheat

- ½ cup shortening
- 1 cup sugar
- 2 eggs
- 1 cup applesauce
- 1 cup whole wheat flour
- 1 cup all-purpose flour
- 3 teaspoons baking powder
- ½ teaspoon salt
- 1 cup chopped nuts

Cream together shortening and sugar in Bosch bowl. Mix in eggs and applesauce. In a separate bowl, stir together the remaining ingredients. Add to the creamed mixture, mixing only enough to moisten flour. Spoon into greased muffin tins, filling each two-thirds full. Bake in a 375° F. oven for 20 to 25 minutes. Serve warm. Makes 2 dozen.

Eight-grain Muffins

Barley, buckwheat, corn, millet, oats, rice, rye, wheat

- ¼ cup barley flour
- ¼ cup buckwheat flour
- ¼ cup corn flour
- ¼ cup millet flour
- ¼ cup oat flour
- ¼ cup rice flour
- ¼ cup rye flour
- ¼ cup wheat flour
- 3 teaspoons baking powder
- ½ teaspoon salt
- 3 eggs
- 1 cup milk
- 2 tablespoons oil
- 3 tablespoons honey

Combine the flours, baking powder, and salt in Bosch bowl. Separate the eggs, reserving whites. Combine the yolks, milk, oil, and honey in Bosch blender bowl. Add to the dry ingredients, and stir only until mixed. Whip egg whites until stiff. Fold into other ingredients. Fill well-greased muffin tins two-thirds full, and bake in a 350° F. oven for 20 to 25 minutes. Makes 10 to 12.

Note: If all of the variety flours are not available, proportions of the other flours may be increased.

Soda Biscuits
Wheat

       2-2¼ **cups whole wheat flour**
         ½ **teaspoon salt**
         ½ **teaspoon baking soda**
         2 **tablespoons shortening**
         1 **cup sour milk or buttermilk**

In the Bosch bowl blend together the whole wheat flour, salt, soda, and shortening until mixture resembles coarse meal. Gently stir in sour milk with a fork, mixing only until all the dry ingredients are moistened. Turn out onto a floured board. Knead two to three times. Sprinkle lightly with flour, and press out with fingers to ½-inch thickness. Cut with a biscuit cutter. Well oil a baking sheet, and dip the top of each biscuit in the oil on the sheet, and then turn over to bake. Bake in a 400° F. oven for 15 minutes or until lightly browned. Makes 12.

> NOTE: Sweet milk may be soured by adding 1 tablespoon cider vinegar to 1 cup sweet milk. Fifty percent all-purpose flour may be used to make a lighter biscuit. After the milk has been added, the dough should be moist. Biscuit dough that is too dry will not make a light biscuit.

Cheese Biscuits

Add shredded cheese and/or minced onion to taste to the dry ingredients.

Double-thick Cheese Biscuits

Prepare Soda Biscuits as directed. Place a small chunk of cheese in the center of half the biscuits, and cover each with an additional biscuit. Seal edges, and bake as directed.

Barley Biscuits
Barley

         3 **cups barley flour**
         ½ **teaspoon salt**
         ¾ **teaspoon baking soda**
       1⅛ **teaspoon cream of tartar**
         4 **tablespoons butter or margarine, softened**
         1 **cup buttermilk**
            Barley flour

Combine the dry ingredients in Bosch bowl. Add butter or margarine, and mix until mixture resembles cornmeal. Stir in buttermilk to form a soft dough, and pour out onto a lightly floured surface. Sprinkle additional barley flour on top of dough, and press down with floured fingers to ½-inch thickness. Cut with a floured biscuit cutter. Bake on a 375° F. greased griddle for 5 minutes or until lightly browned. Makes 12 to 14.

Baking Powder Biscuits
Wheat

         1 **cup all-purpose flour**
         1 **cup whole wheat flour**
         3 **teaspoons baking powder**
         ½ **teaspoon salt**
         4 **tablespoons shortening**
         ¾ **cup milk**

Thoroughly blend flours, baking powder, and salt. Add shortening, and mix until texture resembles coarse meal. Add milk, and stir only until blended. Remove from bowl to a lightly floured board, kneading two to three times or until dough is just pliable. Roll out to ½-inch thickness, and cut with a biscuit cutter. Dip the top of the biscuits in the oil from well-oiled baking sheet, and turn biscuits over. Place in rows with biscuits just touching each other. Bake in a 400° F. oven for 15 minutes or until lightly browned. Makes 12.

Ha'pennies
Wheat

 1 **cup whole wheat flour**
 2 **cups shredded sharp Cheddar cheese**
 ½ **cup butter or margarine, softened**
 4 **tablespoons dehydrated onion flakes**

Combine all the ingredients in the Bosch bowl. Stir until ingredients form a ball. Shape into a roll 1 inch in diameter, and wrap in waxed paper. Refrigerate 2 hours. Cut into ¼-inch slices, place on lightly greased baking sheets, and bake in a 375° F. oven for 10 minutes. Serve as an appetizer or snack. Makes 4 dozen.

Wheat Thins
Wheat

 2½ **cups whole wheat flour**
 1 **teaspoon salt**
 ¼ **cup sugar**
 ½ **cup butter or margarine**
 1 **teaspoon vanilla**
 ¾ **cup water**
   Salt or herb seasoning

Combine the dry ingredients. Add the butter or margarine, and mix until thoroughly blended. Add the vanilla and water, and mix until smooth. Roll out paper-thin on a lightly floured board, or roll directly on a greased baking sheet. (Use the bottom of the baking sheet if the sheet has sides.) Lightly sprinkle with salt or herb seasoning, cut into squares with a pastry wheel, and bake in a 400° F. oven for 5 to 8 minutes or until crisp. If the outer rim browns too quickly, remove the browned sections and return the unfinished portions to the oven. Makes 4 dozen.

Knockbrod

A traditional Swedish recipe made during the harvest season. Originally, it was made with a hole in the center and stored on poles across the ceiling during the winter. The texture resembles a chewy cracker.

Rye

 3¼ **cups rye flour**
 1 **cup buttermilk**
 1 **teaspoon salt**
 1 **teaspoon baking soda**
 ¼ **cup melted butter or margarine**

Pour flour into Bosch bowl. Make a well in the center of the flour, and add the remaining ingredients. Knead only until dough is smooth and stiff. Divide into six equal portions. On a lightly floured surface, roll out each portion to a paper-thin disk about 12 inches in diameter. Wrap dough around a rolling pin, and roll off onto lightly oiled baking sheets. Prick all over with a fork. Bake in a 350° F. oven for 15 to 20 minutes or until lightly browned. Slide onto wire racks to cool. Makes 6.

Honey Graham Crackers
Wheat

 2½ **cups whole wheat flour**
 1 **teaspoon salt**
 1 **teaspoon baking soda**
 ⅓ **cup packed brown sugar**
 ½ **cup shortening**
 ⅓ **cup honey**
 ¼ **cup oil**
 3 **tablespoons cold water**

Blend the flour, salt, baking soda, brown sugar, and shortening in the Bosch bowl. Add honey and oil, and mix again. Add cold water, and mix only enough to combine. Roll out to ⅛-inch thickness on ungreased cookie sheets. Cut into 2-inch squares. Prick crackers with fork. Bake on the center rack in a 425° F. oven for 8 to 10 minutes. If the outside row of crackers browns before the center, remove outer crackers from the pan and continue baking. Makes 7 dozen.

Corn Fritters
Wheat

1 large or 2 small eggs
½ cup milk
2 cups whole wheat flour
2 cups fresh or canned corn, drained
1½ teaspoons salt
⅓ teaspoon pepper
2 teaspoons baking powder
1 tablespoon butter or margarine
Deep-fat cooking oil
Maple syrup (optional)

Beat eggs, and stir in flour and milk. Add remaining ingredients, and blend. Spoon heaping tablespoons of batter into hot, 375° F. cooking oil, and cook until browned, turning once. Drain on paper toweling, and serve hot with maple syrup, if desired. Makes 14 to 16.

Genee's Treat
Wheat

1 cup cooked wheat
1 cup milk
½ teaspoon salt
1 teaspoon honey
1 teaspoon baking powder
2 cups whole wheat flour
Deep-fat cooking oil
Butter, honey, or jam

Mix the first six ingredients until well blended. Shape into small oval rolls, and deep-fat fry in 375° F. oil until golden brown and crisp on each side. Serve hot with butter, honey, or jam. Makes 18 to 20.

> NOTE: One cup of the whole wheat flour may be replaced with ½ cup each of barley and rye flour.

Sopapilla
Wheat

3½ cups whole wheat flour
¼ cup shortening
½ teaspoon salt
1½ cups warm water
Cooking oil

Combine flour and shortening in Bosch bowl. Knead until the shortening and flour are well blended and the texture resembles cornmeal. Add the salt to the warm water, and pour into flour. Knead for 10 minutes, and then cover and let rest 3 to 4 hours or overnight.

Pour 2 inches of oil into a large frying pan, and heat to 375° F. Using as little flour as possible, roll the dough out on a lightly floured surface until paper-thin and approximately 12 inches in diameter. Slowly lower the dough into the hot oil. Dough will sink nearly to the bottom of the pan. As it rises, use a fork to lightly press the dough back under the surface of the hot oil. Repeat over the entire surface of the dough, causing it to balloon. When ballooning has stopped, allow dough to remain in the oil until browned on both sides, turning only once. Remove from oil, and place on paper toweling to drain. Makes 24.

> NOTE: Sopapilla may be enjoyed hot with butter and honey, or top with cooked chicken, stew meat, hamburger, or chopped lamb. A generous spoonful of chili may be poured over the meat. Top with a dollop of sour cream, chopped green onions, sliced radishes, black olives, shredded cheese, and/or corn chips.

Sopapilla Puffs

Using a rolling pin, roll out bread to a large circle. Cut into quarters, and fry as above. Stuff with sandwich filling or serve hot with butter and honey.

Chapati
Wheat

    2 cups whole wheat flour
    ½ teaspoon salt
    ¼ cup butter or margarine
    ¾ cup water
      Sour cream or yogurt (optional)

Blend flour, salt, and butter or margarine in Bosch bowl. Add enough water to make a stiff dough. Knead until smooth and elastic. Cover with a damp cloth, and let rest 30 minutes. Form dough into 1-inch balls. Roll out paper-thin, and bake on a lightly greased griddle. Use as a bread, or generously spread with sour cream or yogurt, and roll up. Makes 20.

Millet or Milo Chapati

Millet or milo flour may be substituted for up to half of the whole wheat flour.

Filled Chapati

Place a tablespoon of leftover vegetable or meat casserole on top of one Chapati, and cover with a second one. Seal the edges, and bake on a lightly greased griddle until done, turning once. Serve with yogurt or sour cream.

Tortillas
Corn, wheat

    1½ cups cornmeal
    1½ cups whole wheat flour
    ¾ teaspoon salt
    3 tablespoons shortening
    ¾ cup warm water

Combine cornmeal, flour, and salt in the Bosch bowl. Cut in shortening until well blended. Add warm water, and stir until mixture is moistened. (A teaspoon or more additional water may be added if dough is too stiff.) Turn out onto a floured surface, and knead 5 minutes or until mixture is no longer sticky. Shape into fourteen balls. Roll each into a thin 6-inch circle. Bake on a hot, ungreased griddle for 1 minute on each side. Makes 14.

Barley Griddle Bread
Barley

    3 cups barley flour
    ¾ teaspoon baking soda
    1¼ teaspoons cream of tartar
    ½ teaspoon salt
    ¼ cup butter or margarine, softened
    1 cup buttermilk

Combine the dry ingredients in the Bosch bowl equipped with wire whips. Add butter or margarine, and cut in until mixture resembles cornmeal. Add sufficient buttermilk to make a soft dough. Turn out onto a lightly floured surface. Roll dough to lightly coat with flour. Dip fingertips in flour and press out dough to a large circle ½-inch in thickness. Cut into 1-inch circles, and bake on a 375° F. greased griddle. Turn once. Serve hot. Makes 1 dozen.

Oatcakes

Oats are the primary grain in Scotland and a staple in the Scots' diet. Their bread takes the form of these oatcakes, rather than loaves. They're served at any meal with butter, jam, or cheese.

Oats

    2 cups rolled oats, quick-cooking or
        old-fashioned
    ¼ teaspoon salt
    ¼ teaspoon baking soda
    ¼ cup buttermilk

Place rolled oats in the Bosch bowl, and blend with wire whips until oats are broken. Add remaining ingredients, and knead ten times. Handle mixture in the same manner as pie dough. If too dry, add a bit more liquid. If too moist, stir in a little flour. Shape into a ball, and roll out to ¼-inch thickness. Cut with a 2-inch cookie cutter or into squares. Bake on a hot, lightly oiled griddle until lightly brown. Serve hot. Makes 12 to 15.

> NOTE: One tablespoon butter and ½ cup water may be used instead of the buttermilk. The addition of an egg and 1 tablespoon of butter gives the oatcake a more tender texture.

Basic Crepes
Wheat

      3 **eggs**
 1½ **cups milk**
      2 **tablespoons butter or margarine, melted**
 1¼ **cups whole wheat flour**
      ¼ **teaspoon salt**

Combine eggs, milk, and melted butter or margarine in Bosch blender. Add flour and salt, and mix until smooth. For more tender crepes, refrigerate batter for 2 to 3 hours or overnight. Pour approximately ⅛ cup batter into a lightly greased and preheated 6-inch frying pan, rotating the pan until the batter covers the bottom surface. Turn over when lightly browned on edges. Crepes may also be prepared with an electric crepe pan. Follow manufacturer's instructions. Makes approximately 24.

Rye Crepes
Substitute 1¼ cups rye flour for the whole wheat flour.

Barley-Wheat Crepes
Reduce whole wheat flour to ¾ cup and add ½ cup barley flour.

Millet-Wheat Crepes
Reduce whole wheat flour to ¾ cup and add ½ cup millet flour.

Oat-Wheat Crepes
Reduce whole wheat flour to ¾ cup and add ½ cup oat flour.

Rice-Wheat Crepes
Reduce whole wheat flour to ¾ cup and add ½ cup rice flour.

Rye-Wheat Crepes
Reduce whole wheat flour to ¾ cup and add ½ cup rye flour.

Milo-Wheat Crepes
Reduce whole wheat flour to ¾ cup and add ¼ cup milo flour.

Buckwheat Crepes
Buckwheat

 ¾ **cup buckwheat flour**
 ¼ **teaspoon salt**
      2 **teaspoons oil**
      2 **eggs**
      1 **cup buttermilk**

Combine flour and salt in a small mixing bowl. Make a well in the center of the flour, and add the remaining ingredients. Blend with a whip until no lumps remain. Cover, and let batter rest at least 30 minutes. For more tender crepes, refrigerate batter for 2 to 3 hours or overnight. Bake as directed for Basic Crepes (left). Makes approximately 12 6-inch crepes.

Cornmeal Crepes
Corn, wheat

 ½ **cup cornmeal**
 ½ **cup hot water**
      3 **eggs**
 ¼ **teaspoon salt**
 ½ **cup whole wheat flour**
      2 **tablespoons butter or margarine, melted**
 ¾-1 **cup milk**

Combine the cornmeal and hot water in a small saucepan. Cook only until cornmeal begins to thicken. Remove from heat, and cool to lukewarm. Mix the cornmeal with the remaining ingredients in the Bosch blender. For more tender crepes, refrigerate batter 2 to 3 hours or overnight. If cornmeal settles to the bottom, blend again. Fry as directed for Basic Crepes (left). Makes 16 6-inch crepes.

Pancake Mix
Wheat

        16 cups whole wheat flour
        ½ cup baking powder
        5 cups nonfat dry powdered milk
        2 tablespoons salt
        2 cups margarine or shortening

Combine the dry ingredients in the Bosch bowl. Using wire whips, cut in margarine or shortening until mixture resembles cornmeal. Store in an airtight container in the refrigerator. Makes 12 batches.

Pancakes

        2 cups Pancake Mix
        1 egg
        1½-2 cups water

Combine Pancake Mix, egg, and water, adjusting water to achieve desired texture. Bake on a hot 375° F. lightly greased griddle until brown. Turn when bubbly. Makes about 15 4-inch pancakes.

Multigrain Pancake Mix

Sure to become a family favorite. Thanks to Joyce Pugh, Magic Mill distributor in Lynden, Washington.

Wheat, oats, corn, buckwheat

        3 cups wheat
        1 cup oat groats
        1 cup corn
        ½ cup buckwheat
        ½ cup soybeans
        1½-2 tablespoons salt
        4 tablepoons baking powder

Grind the wheat, oat groats, corn, buckwheat, and soybeans in the Magic Mill III Plus™. Transfer flours to Bosch bowl. Using the wire whips, mix the grains, and add salt and baking powder. Store in an airtight container. Makes 4 batches.

Multigrain Pancakes

        1 egg
        1½ cups milk
        ¼ cup cooking oil
        ¼ cup applesauce or honey
        2 cups Multigrain Pancake Mix

Combine egg, milk, oil, and applesauce or honey in a 1-quart bowl. Add Multigrain Pancake Mix, and blend only until flour is moistened. Pour out onto a lightly greased 375° F. griddle. Bake until bubbly and brown. Turn once. Makes about 20 4-inch pancakes.

Buttermilk Pancake Mix
Choice of grains

        16 cups whole grain flour*
        4 cups dry powdered buttermilk
        5 tablespoons salt
        ¼ cup baking soda

Combine whole grain flour, dry powdered buttermilk, salt, and baking soda. Store in a covered container. Makes 8 batches.

*Use at least 50 percent whole wheat and a variety of mixed grains for the balance of the flour content.

Buttermilk Pancakes

        2½ cups Buttermilk Pancake Mix
        2 cups water
        2 eggs, beaten
        4 tablespoons oil

Combine Buttermilk Pancake Mix and water. Add beaten eggs and oil. Mix only until blended. Pour onto a lightly greased 375° F. griddle, and bake until bubbly and brown. Turn once. Makes about 20 4-inch pancakes.

Buttermilk Waffles

Prepare Buttermilk Pancakes. Add 2 tablespoons water to batter, and fry on a hot waffle iron.

Country Pancakes

This recipe is easy to memorize. It's a recipe of 2s; every ingredient has a 2 in it!

Barley

- 2 **cups buttermilk**
- 2 **eggs, separated**
- 2 **tablespoons honey**
- 2 **tablespoons melted butter or margarine**
- 2 **cups barley flour**
- 2 **teaspoons baking soda**
- ½ **teaspoon salt**
  Killarney Cream (below)

Blend buttermilk, egg yolks, honey, and melted butter or margarine in a large bowl. Add dry ingredients. In a small bowl, beat egg whites until stiff. Fold into batter. Fry pancakes on a lightly greased 375° F. griddle until golden brown, turning once. Serve with Killarney Cream. Makes about 20 4-inch pancakes.

NOTE: Whole wheat, buckwheat, or rye flour may be substituted for the barley flour. Any combination of barley, rye, wheat, and buckwheat flour is also excellent. Fifty percent millet flour may also be used in combination with any of these grains.

Killarney Cream

- 1 **cup whipping cream**
- 1 **cup sour cream**
- 4 **tablespoons honey**
- 2 **cups sliced fruit**

Whip the sour cream and whipping cream together in a small bowl until soft peaks form. Slowly add the honey. Fold in fruit. Generously spread over pancakes. Makes 4 cups.

Ginger Pancakes

Barley

- 1½ **cups barley flour**
- 1 **teaspoon salt**
- 2 **teaspoons baking powder**
- 2 **tablespoons honey**
- 2 **eggs**
- ⅓ **cup melted butter or margarine**
- 1½ **cups milk**
- 1 **½-inch cube fresh, peeled ginger root**
  Honey or syrup

Stir together flour, salt, and baking powder in a large mixing bowl. Combine honey, eggs, butter or margarine, milk, and ginger root in Bosch blender. Whip until ginger is pureed. Pour into flour mixture. Mix well. Lightly grease griddle, and heat. Sprinkle a few drops of water on griddle to test temperature. When bubbles dance, pour batter into 8-inch circles. Fry until bubbles appear on surface. Turn once. Serve with warm honey or syrup. Makes about 12 8-inch pancakes.

NOTE: One teaspoon ground ginger may be used instead of the fresh ginger root. Whole wheat, oat, buckwheat, and rye flours, or a combination of these grains, may be used instead of the barley flour.

Cinnamon Pancakes

Use 1 teaspoon cinnamon instead of the ginger.

Buckwheat Pancakes

Buckwheat, wheat

- 1½ **cups buckwheat flour**
- ½ **cup whole wheat flour**
- 1 **teaspoon baking soda**
- ½ **teaspoon baking powder**
- ½ **teaspoon salt**
- 2 **teaspoons honey or molasses**
- 2 **tablespoons oil**
- 3 **cups buttermilk**

Combine dry ingredients in a large mixing bowl. Make an indentation in the center of the flour mixture, and pour in honey or molasses, oil, and buttermilk. Stir until smooth. Cover, refrigerate, and let rest for 2 to 3 hours or up to 3 days. Fry on a lightly greased 375° F. griddle until bubbly and browned. Turn once. Makes about 15 4-inch pancakes.

Milo Pancakes

Milo

 2 cups milo flour
 3 teaspoons baking powder
 ¾ teaspoon salt
 ½ cup nonfat dry powdered milk
 3 eggs, separated
 1½-2 cups water

Combine dry ingredients and egg yolks. Add water to achieve pancake batter consistency. Whip egg whites until stiff. Fold into batter. Bake on a hot, 375° F. griddle until golden brown, turning once. Makes about 20 4-inch pancakes.

Apple Milo Pancakes

Wash and core one apple. Peel if desired. Puree in the Bosch blender with ½ cup water. Add 1 teaspoon cinnamon. Pour into a 2-cup measure, and add enough water to equal 1½ cups. Prepare pancakes as directed for Milo Pancakes, substituting the apple mixture for the water.

Rye Pancakes

Rye

 3 eggs, separated
 1⅔ cups buttermilk
 1 teaspoon baking soda
 1½ cups rye flour
 1 tablespoon sugar
 1 teaspoon baking powder
 ½ teaspoon salt
 3 tablespoons butter or margarine, softened

Beat the egg yolks, and add the buttermilk. Combine dry ingredients, and add to the egg yolks and buttermilk. Blend in butter or margarine. Stiffly beat egg whites, and fold into batter. Bake on a hot 375° F. griddle until brown, turning once. Makes about 8 4-inch pancakes.

Eight-grain Waffles

Barley, buckwheat, corn, millet, oats, rice, rye, wheat

 ¼ cup barley flour
 ¼ cup buckwheat flour
 ¼ cup corn flour
 ¼ cup millet flour
 ¼ cup rice flour
 ¼ cup rye flour
 ¼ cup wheat flour
 3 teaspoons baking powder
 1 teaspoon salt
 2 cups milk
 4 tablespoons melted margarine or oil
 2 eggs, separated

Combine dry ingredients in a large bowl. In a separate bowl, blend together milk, melted margarine or oil, and egg yolks. Add liquid ingredients to dry ingredients, and blend. Beat the egg whites until stiff. Fold gently into batter. Bake in a hot waffle iron until brown. Makes 4 10-inch waffles.

NOTE: If all of the specified flours are not available, increase the proportions of the other flours.

Yeast Waffles

Choice of grain

 2 cups warm water or milk
 2 tablespoons honey
 1 tablespoon yeast
 2 tablespoons oil
 ½ teaspoon salt
 2 cups whole grain flour*

Combine water or milk, honey, and yeast in a small mixing bowl. Add oil, salt, and flour. Stir until smooth. Batter should be thin. Allow the batter to rest 15 to 20 minutes or overnight. Bake on a hot, lightly oiled waffle iron until brown. Makes 4 10-inch waffles.

NOTE: Milk may be substituted for the water. Eggs may also be added.

*Wheat, rye, rice, buckwheat, or any combination of these flours is excellent. Barley and oat flours have excellent flavor but do not rise as high. If using, combine with 50 percent wheat, rye, rice, or buckwheat. Use only one-third millet or corn flours and two-thirds other flours, preferably wheat.

A crystal jar of uncooked Canadian Cracked Cereal (page 61) stands behind four ready-to-eat favorites: (clockwise from left) Whole Wheat Cooked Cereal topped with shredded Cheddar cheese (page 62), Breakfast Barley (page 57), Rice 'n Rais (page 61), and Grand Granola (page 6

Cereals

Whole cooked grains have an amazing variety of uses. They form the basis of a hearty breakfast, and thus their cooking instructions are included in this section. However, they also make a delicious light lunch or a satisfying dinner. They can be eaten alone, topped with milk, or used in cookies and snacks. Whether used as whole kernels or in the cracked or rolled form, cooked grains add substance to many dishes.

The art of cooking whole grains is simple. Grain, water, salt, and time are the principal ingredients. Grains are excellent either cooked by themselves or in combinations. Each grain has its own flavor and texture. When you combine grains, a myriad of flavor combinations is at your fingertips. If you do not care for one particular grain by itself, add another grain to it. Corn tends to keep its unique flavor, so be sure that you want corn flavor when adding corn.

Whole Grains

When combining whole grains for a quick-cooking cereal (30 to 40 minutes), use any or all of these grains in the whole kernel form: barley, buckwheat, millet, oats, or rice. When cooked in combination, check the millet for doneness. It takes 5 to 10 minutes longer to cook than the other grains.

Do not combine whole kernel corn, rye, wheat, or milo with the quick-cooking cereal grains. The outer layers of these grains take longer to cook than do the softer grains. After cracking, they may be added to the softer grains. Rolled oats or rolled wheat cook too quickly to add at the beginning of the cooking time. Add them in the last 5 minutes.

Cracked Grains

Cracking reveals the soft endosperm of the grains which enables them to cook more quickly. It also brings a combination of grains to a similar texture. Crack wheat, rye, and corn coarsely. Combine with your choice of whole kernel grains. Use three parts water with one part grain. Cover and cook 30 to 40 minutes. Adjust water content if needed. Cracked grains have a tendency to stick to the bottom of the pan; occasional stirring is necessary. Cracked grains are easily cooked in a double boiler, eliminating the risk of sticking.

Grain/Water Measurements

The charts below give the standard measurements for water, salt, and grain to be used in cooking whole grains.

Buckwheat, corn, oats, rye, rice, and wheat use a standard measurement of two parts water to one part grain.

Yield	1 cup	2 cups	6 cups
Water	¾ cup	1½ cups	4 cups
Salt	¼ teaspoon	⅓ teaspoon	1 teaspoon
Grain	⅓ cup	⅔ cup	2 cups

Barley, millet, corn, and milo use a standard measurement of three parts water to one part grain.

Yield	1 cup	2 cups	6 cups
Water	¾ cup	1½ cups	4½ cups
Salt	⅛ teaspoon	½ teaspoon	¾ teaspoon
Grain	¼ cup	½ cup	1½ cups

Although barley uses the three to one ratio, it can use up to 6 cups of water in cooking.

Cooking Methods for Whole Grains

Energy Saver

The evening before serving, bring salted water to a boil. Add grains, and return mixture to a boil. Cover and turn off heat. The next morning, reheat and serve.

Vacuum Bottle

Pour boiling water into a vacuum bottle to heat the lining. Pour the water out. Add grains, salt, and boiling water. Screw the lid on tightly, and lay the vacuum bottle on its side. Cereal will be ready to eat the following morning.

Rice, millet, and corn do not completely cook using this method.

Gas Range

Combine grains, salt, and boiling water in a covered casserole dish. Place the dish in a gas oven. The pilot light should cook the grains overnight.

Electric Range

Combine grains, salt, and water in a covered casserole dish. Bake overnight at 150° F.

Blanket

Combine grains, salt, and water in a saucepan. Bring to a boil. Cover the pan, and wrap it in newspapers or in a blanket for 2 to 3 hours.

Coal Range

Stoke the fire, and put grains, salt, and water in a covered pan. Place the pan at the back of the stove, off the direct heat, and let sit overnight.

Hot Rocks

Build a fire on the top of ten to twelve large rocks, either outside or in the fireplace. Combine grains, salt, and water in an iron dutch oven. Cover. When rocks are hot and only hot coals remain, spread the rocks to allow room for the dutch oven to be placed in the center. Surround with the hot rocks, and place two to three hot rocks on the lid. Cook grains 30 to 45 minutes or until done.

Slow Cooker

Combine grains, water, and salt in slow cooker, and cook on low overnight.

Hints for Using Breakfast Grain

When cooking whole grains for breakfast, make plenty. Use what you need for breakfast, and save the rest for a chilled salad for the evening meal. Leftover whole grain cereal can also be added to casseroles, soups, bread, and pancakes. Use the suggested cooked grain in a given recipe or select one of your favorites.

Be adventuresome when thinking of whole grains. For example, try eating popped popcorn as a breakfast cereal. It is delicious plain or with milk and honey. Another great morning cereal is raw rolled oats with cream and honey or raisins.

Breakfast Barley
Barley

> 1 **cup barley**
> 3 **cups water**
> ½ **teaspoon salt**

Combine ingredients in a medium saucepan, and bring to a boil. Cover, reduce heat to low, and simmer for 30 minutes. Serves 4 to 6.

> NOTE: For a softer texture, add up to 3 cups additional water, and simmer 30 minutes longer. Stir occasionally.

Buckwheat Cereal
Buckwheat

> 1 **cup buckwheat groats**
> 2-2½ **cups water**
> ½ **teaspoon salt**

Combine all ingredients in a medium saucepan, and bring to a boil. Cover, and simmer 30 minutes. Stir occasionally. Serves 4.

Cornmeal Mush
Corn

> ½ **teaspoon salt**
> 5 **cups hot water**
> 1 **cup cornmeal**
> 2 **cups cold water**
> **Cream and honey (optional)**
> **Shredded Cheddar cheese (optional)**

Bring hot water and salt to a boil in a large saucepan. In a separate bowl, combine cornmeal and cold water. Stir slowly into the hot water. Reduce heat, and let cook 5 to 10 minutes until thickened. Stir often. Serve with cream and honey or top with shredded cheese. Serves 6 to 8.

Fried Mush

Prepare Cornmeal Mush as directed. Pour into a loaf pan, and chill until set, about 1 hour. Cut into ½-inch slices. Fry on a lightly greased griddle for 4 to 5 minutes on each side or until lightly brown. Serve with butter and syrup.

Creamy Millet
Millet

   1 cup millet
   3 cups milk
   ½ teaspoon salt

Combine all ingredients in the top of a double boiler. Cook over simmering water until millet is tender, approximately 45 to 60 minutes. Stir occasionally. Serves 4.

Good Morning Millet Cereal
Millet

   1 cup millet
   3 cups water
   ½ teaspoon salt

Combine all ingredients in a medium saucepan, and bring to a boil. Reduce heat to low, and simmer 30 to 40 minutes. Serves 4.

Milo Cereal
Milo

   1 cup milo
   3 cups water
   ½ teaspoon salt

Combine ingredients in a medium saucepan. Cover and simmer until done, about 1 hour. Serves 4 to 6.

Creamy Milo
Substitute milk for the water. Cook in a double boiler over simmering water for 1½ hours. Stir occasionally.

Cracked Milo Cereal
Milo

   1 cup cracked milo
   3 cups water or milk
   ½ teaspoon salt

Combine ingredients in a medium saucepan. Cover, and simmer until done, approximately 40 minutes. Stir occasionally. Adjust water content, if needed. Serves 4 to 6.

Morning Oats
Oats

   2 cups water
   ½ teaspoon salt
   1 cup oat groats or steel-cut oats

Combine water and salt in a small saucepan, and bring to a boil. Add oats, and reduce heat. Cover and simmer for 30 minutes. Serves 4.

Fruited Oatmeal
Oats

   1½ cups milk
   1½ cups water
   1 teaspoon salt
   1½ cups rolled oats, quick-cooking or
       old-fashioned
   ¾ cup raisins

Combine milk, water, and salt in a 2-quart saucepan. Cover, and bring to a boil. Add oats and raisins. Reduce heat, and simmer 5 minutes or until oats are tender. Serves 4 to 5.

   NOTE: Small pieces of dried apricots, peaches, dates, prunes, pears, or other dried fruits may be substituted for the raisins.

...wn sugar and cream turn Fruited Oatmeal into a breakfast sensation.

Creamy Rolled Oats

Oats

>   1 cup rolled oats, quick-cooking or
>   old-fashioned
>   2 cups cold water
>   ½ teaspoon salt

Combine all ingredients in the top of a double boiler or in a medium saucepan. In a double boiler, cook over boiling water for 20 to 30 minutes. In a saucepan, bring to a boil, and then reduce heat and simmer gently until oats are tender. Stir often. Serves 4.

Flaky Oatmeal

Combine water and salt in medium saucepan, and bring to a boil. Gently stir in rolled oats, and return to a boil. Cover, and remove from heat. Let stand 10 to 15 minutes. Do not stir.

Grand Granola

Oats

>   2 cups rolled oats, quick-cooking or
>   old-fashioned
>   ½ cup slivered almonds
>   1 cup shredded coconut
>   ½ cup sunflower seeds
>   ½ teaspoon salt
>   ¼ cup butter or margarine
>   ¼ cup honey or molasses
>   2 cups raisins

In the Bosch mixing bowl, combine the first five ingredients. Melt butter or margarine and honey together in a small saucepan. Pour over dry ingredients, and blend well. Spread on a baking sheet. Bake in a 300° F. oven for 30 minutes, stirring occasionally. Remove from oven, and add raisins. Makes 6 to 7 cups.

>   NOTE: Diced dates, dried apricots, or dried cherries may be substituted for the raisins. Cashews, walnuts, or other nuts may be used in place of the almonds.

Irene's Granola

Oats, wheat

>   1½ cups oil
>   1½ cups honey
>   5 cups oatmeal
>   1 cup sesame seeds
>   1 cup sunflower seeds
>   1 cup coconut
>   1 cup soy flour
>   1 cup powdered milk
>   1 cup whole wheat flour
>   1 cup slivered almonds

Blend together honey and oil. Add remaining ingredients, and stir well. Bake on large baking sheets in a 300° F. oven for 1 hour. Stir occasionally. Makes 12 cups.

Granola Treats

Prepare Irene's Granola as directed. While still warm, add carob chips, chocolate chips, or butterscotch chips to taste. Stir until melted. Press onto a buttered baking sheet, and let cool. Cut into squares, and serve as a chewy candy.

Baby Bear Porridge

"Just right!"

Oats, wheat

>   2¼ cups water
>   ½ teaspoon salt
>   1 cup rolled oats, quick-cooking or
>   old-fashioned
>   2 tablespoons cracked wheat

Combine water and salt in a medium saucepan, and bring to a boil. Add rolled oats and cracked wheat. Reduce heat, and simmer gently until done. Stir occasionally. Serves 4.

Rice Cereal
Rice

>   2 **cups water**
>   ½ **teaspoon salt**
>   1 **cup brown rice**

Bring water and salt to a boil in a small saucepan. Add rice, and stir only enough to combine. Cover with a heavy lid to prevent steam from escaping. Reduce heat to simmer, and cook 30 to 40 minutes. Do not stir. Taste-test rice kernels for tenderness. Serves 4.

Browned Rice

To serve as a side dish, saute rice in a tablespoon of oil until lightly browned, then prepare as directed.

Rice 'n Raisins
Rice

>   2½ **cups water**
>   ½ **teaspoon salt**
>   1 **cup rice**
>   ½ **cup raisins**

Bring water and salt to a boil in a medium saucepan. Stir in rice. Reduce heat, cover, and simmer for 30 minutes. Add raisins, and continue simmering until rice is tender. Serves 4 to 6.

>   NOTE: Cinnamon and sugar to taste may be added along with the raisins.

Toddler's Delight
Rice, barley

>   1 **cup rice**
>   ½ **cup barley**
>   **Water**
>   **Salt**

Crack the rice and barley to a meal texture in the Magic Mill III Plus™. Store in a small, airtight container. To cook, use 3 tablespoons cracked grain to 1 cup water. Bring water and ½ teaspoon salt to a boil in a small saucepan. Sprinkle the cracked grains over the water, and stir. Turn off heat, and cover pan. Let stand 5 minutes. Serves 2.

Rye Cereal
Rye

>   2 **cups water**
>   ½ **teaspoon salt**
>   1 **cup rye**

Combine salt and water in a small saucepan. Bring to a boil. Add rye, and cover. Reduce heat, and let simmer for 1 hour. Serves 4.

Cracked Rye

Coarsely crack the rye in the Magic Mill III Plus™. Prepare as directed, substituting 1 cup cracked rye for the whole kernel rye. Cook 15 to 20 minutes.

Canadian Cracked Cereal
Rye, wheat

>   1 **cup rye**
>   1 **cup whole wheat**
>   ¼ **cup flax seed**
>   **Water**
>   **Salt**

Coarsely crack the rye and wheat in the Magic Mill III Plus™. Add flax seed. Mix thoroughly. Store in a covered container. To cook, use 1 cup cereal to 3 cups water. Bring water and ½ teaspoon salt to a boil in a medium saucepan. Add grains, and stir. Cover, and reduce heat to low. Let cook 20 minutes or until soft. Stir often. Serves 2 to 4.

Whole Wheat Cooked Cereal
Wheat

> 1 cup wheat
> 2 cups water
> ½ teaspoon salt

Method 1: Combine wheat, water, and salt in a small saucepan. Bring to a boil, and then reduce heat to low. Cover, and simmer for 2 to 3 hours, adding additional water if needed.
Method 2: Combine wheat, water, and salt in a 1-quart casserole dish. Cover, and bake in a 150° F. oven for 6 hours or overnight. Serves 4.

Cracked Wheat Cereal

Coarsely crack the wheat kernels. Prepare the cereal as directed. Simmer 15 to 20 minutes.

Toasted Cracked Wheat Cereal

Coarsely crack the wheat kernels, and then lightly toast in a 350° F. oven for 15 to 20 minutes. Prepare as directed for Cracked Wheat. Cereal will have a toasty flavor.

Four-grain Cereal
Rye, wheat, rice, millet

> ½ cup rye
> ½ cup whole wheat
> ½ cup brown rice
> ½ cup millet
> 4½ cups water
> 1 teaspoon salt

Combine all ingredients in a 2-quart casserole. Cover, and bake overnight in a 150° F. oven. Serves 6 to 8.

> NOTE: Barley, oats, and/or buckwheat may be substituted for the above grains.

Creamy and Crunchy Cereal
Choice of grains

> ½ cup cracked grains
> ¼ cup butter or margarine
> ⅓ cup honey
> 1½ cups water or milk
> ½ cup raisins or other dried fruit
> ¼ cup nuts or seeds

In a medium saucepan, melt the butter or margarine over low heat. Add cracked grains. Saute grain until it begins to change color. Add honey and water or milk. Stir until grain is evenly distributed. Cover, and simmer 4 to 5 minutes, stirring occasionally. Add raisins or other dried fruits and nuts or seeds. Serves 4.

Breakfast Medley
Oats, barley, buckwheat, wheat, rice, rye, millet

> ½ cup oats
> ½ cup barley
> ½ cup buckwheat
> ½ cup whole wheat
> ½ cup brown rice
> ¼ cup rye
> ¼ cup millet
> 6 tablespoons flax seed
>   Water
>   Salt

Combine grains in a large bowl. Store in an airtight container. To cook, use 1½ cups grain mixture to 4 cups water. Bring water and ½ teaspoon salt to a boil in a 2-quart saucepan. Add grain mixture. Return to a boil, cover, and turn off heat. Let grains soften overnight. The following morning, bring back to a boil and simmer on low for 15 minutes. Serves 6 to 8.

> NOTE: To reduce cooking time, crack grains and prepare using the same proportions as above. Cook 15 to 20 minutes, stirring occasionally, as cracked cereal has a tendency to stick. If necessary, add more water.

Soups and Salads

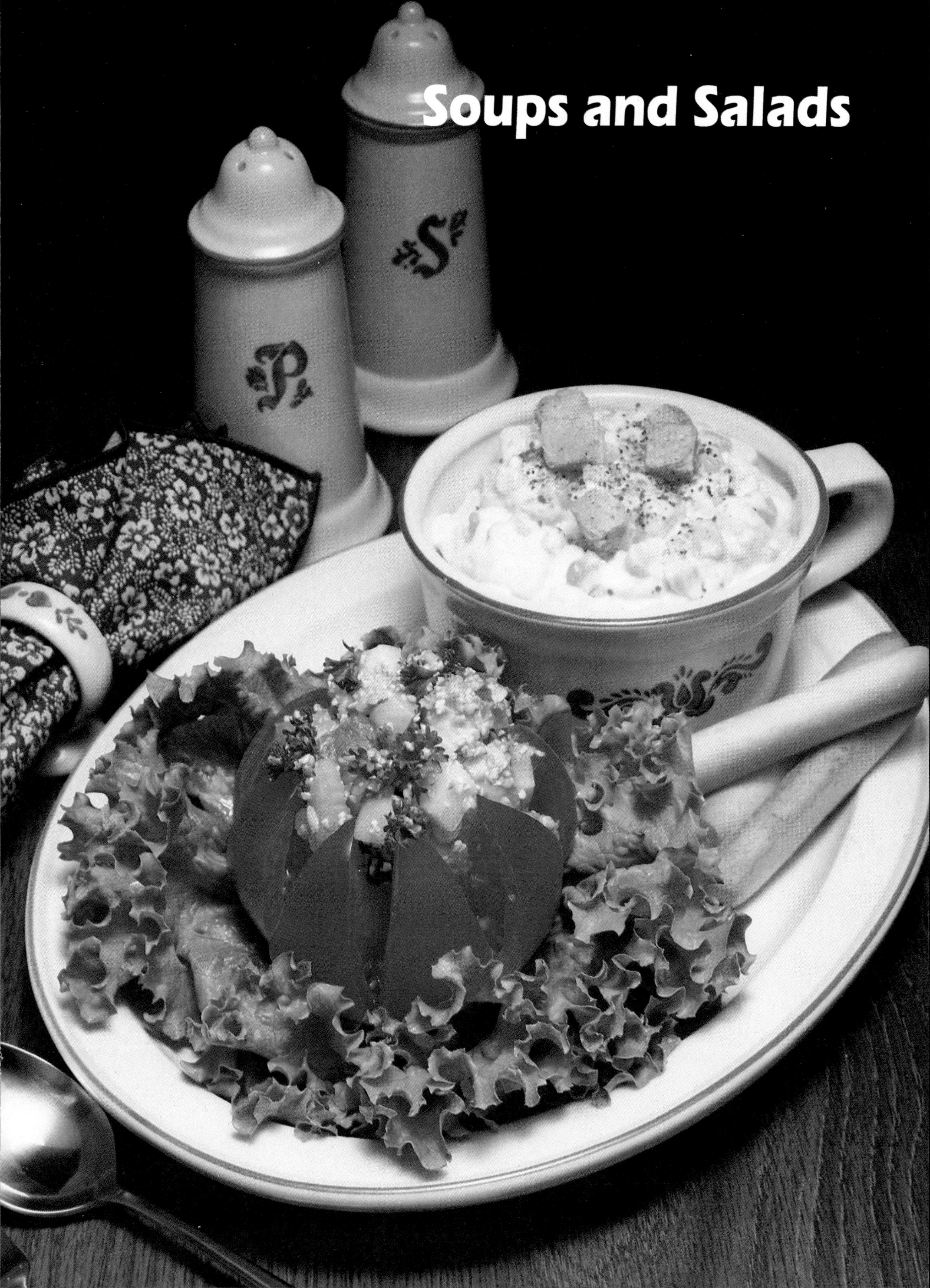

Soups and Salads

Grains are a naturally good addition to soups and stews. They make stew more hearty and soup a satisfying meal in itself. While adding flavor and nutritional value, they also serve as a thickening agent.

When adding dry grains, remember that raw grain absorbs nearly twice its volume in moisture. Add additional water or juice to the soup. Cooking time is also a prime consideration. Some whole grains simply take too long to cook. They should be precooked or cracked before adding.

Cooked grains also make a quick and filling salad. The recipes in this book and your own imagination will get you away from thinking of salads as only lettuce and tomatoes.

Start with cooked grains, perhaps some left over from breakfast. Add shredded carrots, chopped celery, green onion, and julienne luncheon meat or cheese. Moisten with salad dressing, and serve on a lettuce leaf.

Try a grain salad with tuna or shrimp, sprouts and water chestnuts. Dress with mayonnaise, and season to taste. Garnish with tomatoes.

Salad recipes are easily adapted to cooked grains. The grains add a chewy texture and enhance the flavor of the green, leafy vegetables.

Danish Soup
Barley

- 1 quart water
- 1 pound lean ground beef
- 2 teaspoons chicken bouillon granules
- 1 teaspoon beef bouillon granules
- 1 quart water
- 6 carrots, peeled and diced
- 5 medium potatoes, peeled and diced
- 1 onion, chopped
- 2 stalks celery, sliced diagonally
- 1 8-ounce can tomato sauce
- 3 tablespoons parsley
- 1 teaspoon salt
- ½ teaspoon pepper
- ⅓ cup barley

Bring 1 quart of water to a boil in a large kettle. Break ground beef into bite-size pieces, and add. Stir in chicken and beef bouillon. Reduce heat, and simmer 10 minutes. Refrigerate until grease hardens on water. Skim off fat, and return to heat. Add the additional 1 quart water and the remaining ingredients. Cook soup 30 minutes or until vegetables and barley are tender. Add more water during cooking if needed. Serves 8 to 10.

Salmon-Buckwheat Chowder
Buckwheat, wheat

- ⅓ cup buckwheat
- ⅔ cup water
- ½ cup chopped onion
- ½ cup chopped celery
- 3 tablespoons butter or margarine
- 2 cups cauliflowerets
- 1 cup peeled and diced potatoes
  Water
- 1 15½-ounce can salmon
- 3 tablespoons whole wheat flour
- 3 cups milk
- 10 ounces frozen peas
- ¾ teaspoon dill weed
  Salt and pepper
- 1 cup shredded sharp cheese

In a medium saucepan, simmer the buckwheat in the ⅔ cup water until tender, 30 to 40 minutes. Set aside. In a large kettle, saute the onion and celery in the butter or margarine. Add cauliflowerets and diced potatoes. Simmer in just enough water to cover vegetables. Remove skin and bones from the salmon, break into chunks, and add to the vegetables. Mix the flour with a few tablespoons of the milk. Add to the vegetables. Add the buckwheat, remaining milk, peas, and dill weed. Salt and pepper to taste. Heat thoroughly. Add shredded cheese, and stir until cheese melts. Serves 8.

Corn Chowder

Corn

        5-6 **tablespoons dried sweet corn**
        1½ **cups water**
          2 **diced potatoes**
          1 **tablespoon honey**
         ¼ **pound bacon, diced**
          1 **small onion, chopped**
          1 **teaspoon salt**
            Pepper
          1 **tablespoon flour**
          1 **cup whole milk**

In a large kettle, simmer corn in water for 1 hour. Add potatoes and honey. Fry the bacon in a small skillet. Drain, reserving 2 tablespoons bacon grease. Saute onion in bacon grease. Add bacon and onion to corn mixture. Simmer until potatoes are tender. Season with salt and pepper. Combine flour and milk, and add to soup. Simmer, and stir until soup thickens. Serves 4.

Chili Basics

Corn, wheat

          6 **dried red chili peppers**
          4 **cups water**
          3 **pounds ground beef**
          3 **pounds ground chuck**
          8 **cloves garlic, minced**
          3 **medium onions, chopped**
          4 **teaspoons salt**
         ½ **teaspoon black pepper**
         ½ **teaspoon allspice**
          3 **tablespoons cumin seed**
          1 **tablespoon oregano**
          8 **tablespoons chili powder**
          2 **tablespoons paprika**
          3 **tablespoons vinegar**
          2 **10½-ounce cans beef consommé**
          2 **cups tomato juice**
          2 **tablespoons whole wheat flour**
          3 **tablespoons corn flour**

Stem and seed the red chili peppers. Cook in water for 30 minutes. Let cool. Brown the meat in a large skillet. Drain off excess fat. Add the garlic and onions, and cook until nearly translucent. Stir in spices and seasonings. Add the water from the peppers a little at a time as needed. Simmer slowly. Add vinegar and consommé. In a small bowl, combine the tomato juice and flours. Blend well, and add to the chili. Simmer 1 to 2 hours. Alter spices to taste. Makes approximately 6 quarts.

> NOTE: If chili peppers are unavailable, add an additional 5 to 6 tablespoons dried chili powder.

Bean Chili

Add 1 quart cooked beans to 2 quarts Chili Basics. Simmer several hours until flavors blend.

Grain Chili

Add 1 quart cooked whole grains to 2 quarts Chili Basics. Simmer several hours until flavors blend.

Pumpkin Soup

Millet

          8 **cups peeled and cubed raw pumpkin**
          3 **tomatoes, peeled and quartered**
          3 **potatoes, diced**
          5 **cups water**
          4 **tablespoons uncooked millet**
          1 **tablespoon butter or margarine**
            Salt and pepper
       ¼-½ **cup cream**

Combine the pumpkin, tomatoes, potatoes, water, and uncooked millet in a large kettle. Cover, and simmer until pumpkin is soft. Mash with a potato masher or puree in blender until smooth. Return to kettle and reheat. Add the butter or margarine. Salt and pepper to taste. Remove from heat, and add cream. Serves 8.

> NOTE: Rice, buckwheat, whole oats, or barley may be used in place of the millet.

Chili Excellente

Millet, wheat

        5 cups dry beans, reds, pinks, or pintos
          Water
      1-2 46-ounce cans tomato juice
        1 cup millet
        4 pounds ground beef
        6 onions, chopped
        1 small bunch celery, chopped
        1 large green pepper, chopped
        4 teaspoons chili powder
        1 teaspoon allspice
        4 tablespoons salt
      2½ teaspoons cumin powder
      ½-1 cup cracked wheat (optional)

Soak beans overnight in 10 cups of cold water. In the morning, drain off water, and add 8 to 10 cups fresh water. Simmer beans until nearly tender, approximately 1½ hours. Add tomato juice as needed. Add the millet, and cook until beans and millet are completely tender. Partially fry the ground beef in a large skillet. Drain off fat. Add to beans and millet. Add chopped onions, celery, green pepper, remaining tomato juice, and spices. Simmer several hours until flavors are well blended. If chili is too thin, add ½ to 1 cup cracked wheat and continue simmering until wheat is tender. Makes approximately 8 quarts.

French Onion Soup

Wheat

        4 tablespoons butter or margarine
        4 yellow onions, chopped
        4 tablespoons whole wheat flour
        5 beef bouillon cubes
        5 cups hot water
          Salt and pepper
        1 bay leaf
        4 slices whole wheat bread
        1 cup shredded longhorn cheese

In a 2-quart kettle, melt butter or margarine, and add onions. Cook slowly over medium heat for 15 minutes or until onions are brown, stirring occasionally. Stir in flour. Dissolve bouillon cubes in hot water. Add bouillon, salt and pepper to taste, and bay leaf. Cover and simmer for 30 minutes. Remove bay leaf. Toast whole wheat bread. Cut each slice into six pieces. Divide bread evenly among four oven-proof soup bowls. Ladle the onion soup over the bread, and generously sprinkle the shredded cheese over the soup. Place under oven broiler until cheese is bubbly. Serve at once. Serves 4.

Three-grain Stew

Wheat, corn, rye

        1 pound beef stew cubes
        4 tablespoons oil
        2 quarts water
        4 tablespoons cracked wheat
        5 tablespoons cracked corn
        4 tablespoons cracked rye
        1 large onion, chopped
      3-4 carrots, peeled and diced
        2 stalks celery, diced
        1 large turnip, peeled and diced
      2-3 teaspoons salt
          Pepper

Brown the meat in the oil in a large kettle. Add the water, cover, and simmer for 1 hour. Allow to cool, and then refrigerate until the fat hardens on top of the water. Skim off fat. Add the grains and vegetables, and simmer until they are tender. Add water during cooking if needed. Season to taste with salt and pepper. Serves 4 to 6.

, wheat, and rye make Three-grain Stew hearty, budget-stretching, and palate-pleasing.

Barley Luncheon Salad
Barley

1 cup diced cooked ham, chicken, turkey,
   tuna, or shrimp
2 cups cooked barley
½ cup chopped onion
½ cup cubed longhorn cheese
1 cup chopped celery
1 cup raw peas, fresh or frozen
½ cup cooked asparagus pieces
1 teaspoon salt
¾ cup salad dressing or mayonnaise
   Lettuce leaves
   Tomato wedges

Combine the first nine ingredients in a large bowl. Refrigerate until well chilled. Serve on lettuce leaves and garnish with tomato wedges. Serves 6.

NOTE: Other grains may be substituted for the barley. Vegetables may be varied according to preference and availability.

New England Buckwheat-Rice Salad
Buckwheat, rice

½ cup buckwheat
½ cup rice
2 cups water
½ teaspoon salt
1 cup mayonnaise
2 tablespoons prepared mustard
1 teaspoon horseradish
2 cups shredded cabbage
½ cup shredded carrot
½ small onion, minced
1 12-ounce can corned beef, cubed
   Salt and pepper
   Lettuce leaves

Combine buckwheat, rice, water, and salt in a medium saucepan. Cook until tender and water is absorbed. Chill. Combine the next seven ingredients in a medium bowl. Mix with the chilled grains. Salt and pepper to taste. Serve on lettuce leaves. Serves 8.

Fiesta Salad
Corn

1 head romaine lettuce
6 green onions, sliced
3 tomatoes, wedged
½ cup cooked whole kernel corn, canned,
   frozen, or fresh
1 avocado, sliced
8 olives, sliced
2 cups corn chips
1 cup grated cheese
2 cups Chili Excellente (page 67)

Tear the lettuce into bite-size pieces, and place in the bottom of a large salad bowl. Layer all the remaining ingredients except the chili. Heat chili to boiling. Just before serving, pour chili over all, and toss well. Serve immediately. Serves 6 to 8.

Corn Salad
Corn

2 12-ounce cans whole kernel corn, drained,
   or 3 cups fresh cooked corn
1 large cucumber, peeled and diced
3 green onions, sliced
2 small tomatoes, chopped
2 tablespoons mayonnaise
3 tablespoons sour cream
1 tablespoon cider vinegar
½ teaspoon salt
¼ teaspoon dry mustard
½ teaspoon celery seed
   Lettuce leaves or tomato cups

Layer the corn, cucumber, onions, and tomatoes in a large salad bowl. Combine the mayonnaise and sour cream. Add the remaining ingredients, and blend well. Toss with the vegetables. Refrigerate until well chilled. Serve on lettuce leaves or in hollowed-out tomato cups. Serves 4 to 6.

Millet Salad
Millet

    2 cups cooked millet
    1 cup cooked pinto beans
    1 cucumber, peeled and diced
    1 cup fresh, frozen or reconstituted
        green peas
    ½ red or green pepper, diced
    1 large carrot, shredded
  ½-1 cup mayonnaise
      Lettuce leaves
      Tomato wedges
      Raw onion rings

Combine the first seven ingredients, and chill thoroughly. Serve on lettuce leaves, and garnish with tomato wedges and onion rings. Serves 6.

Shrimp Salad
Rice, millet

  2½ cups water
    ⅔ cup brown rice
    ⅓ cup millet
    ½ teaspoon salt
    ½ dill pickle, chopped
    1 tablespoon chopped onion
    2 4½-ounce cans shrimp
    1 cup fresh or frozen raw peas
    ¾ cup mayonnaise
    1 avocado
      Lettuce leaves
      Tomato wedges

Bring the water to a boil in a medium saucepan. Add the rice, millet, and salt, and cook until grain is tender and water is absorbed. Allow to cool. Add the dill pickle, onion, shrimp, peas, and mayonnaise. Mix lightly with a fork. Chill thoroughly. Just before serving, peel and slice the avocado. Toss with salad. Serve on lettuce leaves, and garnish with tomato wedges. Serves 6.

> NOTE: Cracked wheat or cracked rye may be substituted for the rice. A combination of wheat, rye, and rice may also be used.

Tabouli
Wheat

    1 cup cracked wheat
  2¾ cups hot water
    ½ cup olive oil
    ¾ cup lemon juice
    5 green onions, chopped
    2 cloves garlic, minced
    ⅛ bunch fresh parsley, chopped
    ½ cup mint leaves, chopped (optional)
    2 large tomatoes, chopped
    6 stalks celery, chopped
    2 small cucumbers, chopped
      Salt and pepper

Combine wheat and hot water, and let soak for 2 to 3 hours. Drain any remaining water. Mix wheat with olive oil and lemon juice. In a large glass bowl, layer half the ingredients as listed, beginning with the wheat. Salt and pepper to taste. Repeat with remaining ingredients. Chill 24 hours. Toss salad before serving. Serves 4 to 6.

Sour Cream Coleslaw
Wheat, rye

    4 cups coarsely shredded cabbage
    ½ cup chopped green pepper
  1½ cups cooked wheat and/or rye
    ¾ cup mayonnaise or salad dressing
    1 cup sour cream
    2 teaspoons celery seed
    3 teaspoons brown sugar
    ½ lemon, juiced

Combine all ingredients in a large bowl. Chill thoroughly before serving. Serves 4.

Tostada Salad

Choice of grain

1 pound ground beef
1 individual-serving-size envelope dry
    onion soup mix
¾ cup water
1 cup cooked grain
½ cup sliced black olives
1 large tomato, chopped
¼ cup chopped green pepper
1 head lettuce, torn into small pieces
1 small onion, sliced
1 cup shredded Monterey Jack cheese
    Black olives
    Tomato wedges

Brown ground beef in a large skillet. Add soup mix, water, and grain. Simmer 10 minutes. While simmering, combine olives, tomato, green pepper, lettuce, and onion. Prepare portions on salad plates. Top with hamburger mixture. Sprinkle with shredded cheese and garnish with black olives and tomato wedges. Serves 6 to 8.

Cabbage-Pepper Slaw

Wheat, rye

4 cups coarsely shredded cabbage
½ cup chopped green pepper
1½ cups cooked wheat and/or rye
1 teaspoon salt
2 tablespoons sugar
1 teaspoon celery seed
2 tablespoons tarragon vinegar
1 teaspoon prepared mustard
½ cup salad dressing or mayonnaise

Combine all ingredients in a large bowl. Chill thoroughly before serving. Serves 4.

Carrot-Pineapple Coleslaw

Add 3 finely shredded carrots and 1 cup drained and crushed pineapple to the Cabbage-Pepper Slaw.

Lettuce Wedges

Choice of grain

½ cup cooked cracked grain
1 cup mayonnaise
¼ cup catsup
¼ cup minced onion
¼ cup chopped green pepper
1 hard-boiled egg, chopped
    Seasoned salt
    Celery salt
    Salt
1 head iceberg lettuce

To prepare dressing, combine grain, mayonnaise, catsup, minced onion, green pepper, and hard-boiled egg. Season to taste with seasoned salt, celery salt and salt. Cut lettuce into wedges. Serve dressing over wedges. Serves 4 to 6.

Grains find their way into three out-of-the-ordinary main dishes: (clockwise from top left) Barley-stuffed Pita Bread (page Pork Chops and Rye (page 76), and Ham and Chicken Crepes (page

Main Dishes

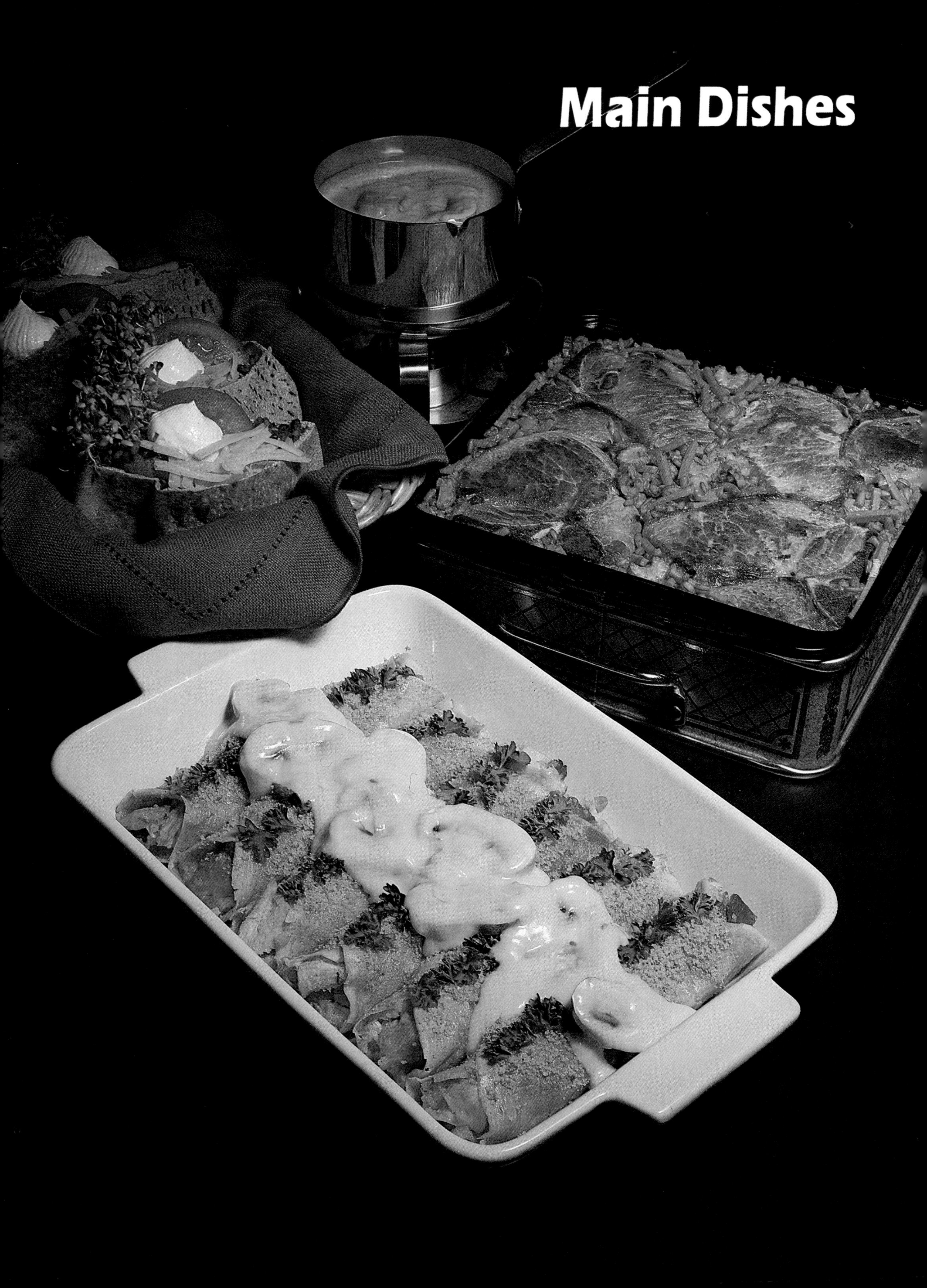

Main Dishes

The unique flavors and textures of grains enhance the meats used in main dishes. As you become acquainted with the different grain flavors, you will be able to substitute or combine grains in your own recipes with some surprisingly good results.

The main dish recipes included in this book begin with casseroles, both oven-baked and skillet. They are followed by hearty main dish toppings which are served over rice or other whole grains. Finally, specialty main dishes are given, all of which include a whole grain or grain flour.

Many of the recipes in the next section of this book, side dishes, can be converted to main dishes by the addition of meat, poultry, or fish. Instead of the usual pasta and potatoes, cooked grains make delicious side dishes to complement meat or poultry. In fact, combining cooked grains with vegetables adds flavor and texture to side dishes. Pilafs and grain casseroles are excellent choices to add interest to a meal. Add cooked vegetables, nuts, seeds, sprouts, or cheese to cooked grains to spice up one side of the dinner plate.

Cooking time is an important concern when using grains in main and side dishes. For example, it is best to avoid combining a grain such as whole wheat, which requires a baking time of 6 hours, with whole rice, which only requires 30 to 40 minutes to cook. Whole wheat, rye, and triticale require long-term cooking. Whole rice, barley, millet, buckwheat, and oats are quick-cooking grains.

The water content required by grains also varies. Uncooked grains will absorb at least twice their volume in water. Millet and barley will absorb more water than other grains.

Cracking grains shortens their cooking time. Cracked wheat and rye take about 20 minutes to cook. Cracked sweet corn requires 1 hour. Cornmeal may be the easiest form of corn to use in casseroles because of the minimal cooking time.

If cooking grains for breakfast, cook extra. When preparing a whole-grain dish for the evening meal, the body of the casserole is already cooked and ready to use.

Barley Skillet Casserole
Barley

½	pound ground beef
½	small onion, chopped
2	sticks celery, chopped
½	cup uncooked barley
2½	cups water
1	teaspoon sweet basil
1	bay leaf
	Salt

Brown the ground beef in a medium skillet. Drain off fat. Add the onion and celery, and saute until the onion is translucent. Add barley, and brown lightly. Add water, basil, and bay leaf. Salt to taste. Cover, and simmer slowly until barley is tender, approximately 50 minutes. Stir occasionally. Serves 2 to 4.

NOTE: Any uncooked grain may be used instead of the barley. Other meats may be substituted for the ground beef. For a vegetarian casserole, beef may be omitted and 3 bouillon cubes used for the flavoring. If using bouillon cubes, saute the onion and celery in a tablespoon of cooking oil.

Tortilla Casserole
Corn

1	pound ground beef
1	large onion, chopped
½	teaspoon chili powder
2	8-ounce cans tomato sauce
2	cups canned, frozen, or fresh whole kernel corn
10-12	Tortillas (page 50)
2	cups shredded Cheddar cheese

In a large skillet, fry ground beef until lightly brown. Add chopped onion, and saute. Add chili powder, tomato sauce, and corn. Grease a 9 x 13-inch baking dish. Arrange five or six tortillas on the bottom of the pan; cover with half the filling. Layer remaining tortillas, sauce, and cheese. Bake in a 350° F. oven for 25 minutes. Serves 6.

Spanish Zucchini
Millet

    ⅔ cup millet
    2 cups water
    ½ teaspoon salt
    3 medium zucchini
      Water
    1 7-ounce can whole green chilies, seeded
      and coarsely chopped
  1½ cups shredded Monterey Jack cheese
    1 large tomato, thinly sliced
      Salt
    1 pint sour cream
    1 teaspoon oregano
    1 teaspoon garlic salt
    ¼ cup chopped green pepper
    ½ cup chopped green onion
    2 tablespoons chopped parsley

In a medium saucepan, combine millet, 2 cups water, and salt. Cover, and cook over medium heat for 45 minutes. Thinly slice the zucchini and place in a second saucepan. Cook in a small amount of salted water until crisp-tender. Set aside. Drain any remaining water from millet. Spread millet in a 3-quart buttered casserole dish, and cover with chilies. Sprinkle half of the cheese on top of the chilies. Drain zucchini, and arrange slices over cheese. Add tomato slices. Sprinkle with salt. In a small bowl, combine sour cream, oregano, garlic salt, green pepper and green onion. Spoon evenly over tomatoes. Sprinkle with remaining cheese. Bake in a 350° F. oven for 30 to 35 minutes or until heated through. Garnish with parsley, and serve immediately. Serves 5 to 6.

NOTE: Any other grain may be substituted for the millet.

Chicken-Millet Casserole
Millet

    2 tablespoons butter or margarine
    ½ large onion, chopped
    1 clove garlic, minced
    ⅔ cup millet
    1 10½-ounce can beef broth
    2 cups chopped cooked chicken

Melt the butter or margarine in a medium skillet, and saute the onion and garlic. Add millet, and brown lightly. Stir in beef broth and chicken. Pour into a 2-quart casserole dish. Cover, and bake in a 350° F. oven for 45 minutes or until millet is tender. Occasionally check moisture content. Serves 6.

NOTE: Two bouillon cubes and 1⅓ cups water may be substituted for the can of beef broth. Milo, rice, cracked wheat, rye, or buckwheat may be used in place of the millet. Slivered almonds, water chestnuts, or mushrooms may be added.

Millet Continental
Millet

    1 pound ground beef
    1 medium onion, chopped
    3 stalks celery, chopped
    1 cup millet
    1 10½-ounce can cream of mushroom soup
  2½ cups water
    ½ cup sunflower seeds
    ½ teaspoon garlic powder
    1 teaspoon salt
    ¼ teaspoon pepper
    ¾ teaspoon poultry seasoning

Brown meat in a large skillet. Drain fat, reserving 2 tablespoons. Transfer meat to a 9 x 13-inch baking dish. Saute onion and celery in remaining fat. Add to the meat. Pour millet over meat mixture. Combine soup, water, sunflower seeds, garlic powder, salt, pepper, and poultry seasoning in a separate bowl. Spread evenly over millet, and mix lightly. Bake in a 350° F. oven for 1 hour or until millet is tender. Serves 6 to 8.

NOTE: Other grains may be substituted for the millet. Reduce water when using other grains.

Chinese Millet Casserole
Millet

     1 **pound ground sausage**
     1 **large onion, chopped**
     1 **small bunch celery and leaves, chopped**
     1 **cup millet**
     2 **individual-serving-size envelopes chicken noodle soup**
     4 **cups boiling water**
     4 **ounces slivered almonds**

Fry sausage over medium-high heat until browned. Transfer to a 9 x 13-inch baking dish. Drain all but 2 to 3 tablespoons of fat from skillet. Saute onion and celery. Add millet, and brown lightly. Pour vegetables and millet over sausage. Combine soup and water in skillet. Pour over meat, vegetables, and millet. Stir to combine. Sprinkle slivered almonds on top. Bake in a 350° F. oven for 45 minutes. Serves 6 to 8.

Spanish Rice
Rice

     ¼ **cup butter or margarine**
     ½ **cup chopped onion**
     ⅓ **cup sliced green pepper**
     1 **cup brown rice**
     1 **cup diced, cooked pork, lamb or beef**
    1½ **cups hot water**
     2 **8-ounce cans tomato sauce**
     1 **teaspoon salt**
        Pepper
        Chili powder (optional)

Melt the butter or margarine in a large skillet. Lightly brown the onion, green pepper, rice, and meat. Add the hot water, tomato sauce, salt, a dash of pepper, and chili powder to taste. Cover, reduce heat to low, and simmer until rice is tender, about 30 minutes. Stir occasionally. Serves 4.

Seven-layer Casserole
Rice

     1 **cup brown rice**
     1 **cup whole kernel canned corn**
     ½ **teaspoon salt**
     2 **8-ounce cans tomato sauce**
    1¾ **cups water**
     ½ **cup chopped onion**
     1 **pound ground beef**
    4-5 **strips bacon**

Spread the brown rice in the bottom of a greased 2-quart casserole dish. Add the canned corn, salt, and one can tomato sauce. Do not stir. Pour 1½ cups water over tomato sauce. Continue layering chopped onion, uncooked ground beef, and additional can of tomato sauce. Pour remaining ¼ cup water over sauce. Place strips of bacon on top. Cover, and bake in a 350° F. oven for 1 hour. Uncover, and bake 30 minutes longer. Additional water may be added if necessary. Serves 6.

Sausage and Rice Casserole
Rice

     1 **pound ground sausage**
     1 **medium onion, chopped**
     4 **stalks celery, diced**
     1 **can beef consomme**
     1 **can cream of mushroom soup**
     1 **cup water**
     1 **cup rice**
        Slivered almonds (optional)

In a large skillet, fry sausage until lightly brown. Add onion and celery, and continue frying until sausage is cooked. Drain off fat. Add remaining ingredients, and mix well. Pour into a 3-quart casserole dish, and bake uncovered in a 350° F. oven for 1 hour or until rice is tender. Top with slivered almonds if desired. Serves 6 to 8.

Seven-layer Casserole is a family favorite that's elegant enough for company b

Chicken Breasts in Rice
Rice

2 chicken breasts, halved and skinned
1 can cream of chicken soup
1 can cream of mushroom soup
1 13-ounce can evaporated milk
1 cup rice
1 package dry onion soup mix

Place chicken breasts in a lightly buttered 9 x 9-inch baking dish. In a separate bowl, combine chicken soup, mushroom soup, evaporated milk, and rice. Mix well. Pour over chicken breasts, and top with dry onion soup mix. Bake in a 350° F. oven for 1 hour or until chicken is done and grain is tender. Serves 4.

Chicken Tetrazzini
Rice, millet, wheat

1 3-pound cut-up fryer chicken
  Water
½ cup millet
½ cup rice
4 teaspoons butter or margarine
1 green pepper, chopped
1 medium onion, chopped
1 4-ounce can sliced mushrooms
4 tablespoons whole wheat flour
2 cups whole milk
  Salt and pepper
½ pound Cheddar cheese
½ pound processed cheese

Place chicken in a large kettle, and cover with water. Simmer until tender. Remove chicken from stock, and cool. Remove meat from bones, and cut into small pieces. Set aside. Add enough water to increase stock to 4 cups. Stir millet and rice into chicken stock, and cook until tender. Melt butter or margarine in a large skillet. Add green pepper, onion, and mushrooms. Saute until tender. Add flour, and blend. Stir in milk, and cook until thickened. Combine chicken and grains with sauce in skillet. Salt and pepper to taste, and add cheeses. Stir until cheeses melt. Pour into a 2-quart casserole dish, and bake in a 350° F. oven for 30 minutes. Serves 6.

Pork Chops and Rye
Rye

1 10½-ounce can onion soup
¾ cup water
¾ cup rye
4 thick pork chops
2 tablespoons oil
  Salt and pepper
3 medium carrots
1 cup thinly sliced celery
¼ teaspoon dried marjoram
⅛ teaspoon oregano
⅛ teaspoon pepper

Combine soup, water, and rye in a medium saucepan. Stir with a fork. Cover, and simmer 30 minutes or until rye has absorbed the liquid. Trim fat from pork chops. Add oil to a large skillet, and brown the pork chops. Season with salt and pepper. Cut carrots into short, thin strips resembling match sticks, and add to the rye. Stir in celery, marjoram, oregano, and pepper. Place rye mixture into a 6 x 10-inch baking dish, and top with the pork chops. Cover, and bake in a 350° F. oven for 1 hour. Serves 4.

Chili Relleno Casserole
Wheat

½ pound lean ground beef
1 medium onion, chopped
½ teaspoon salt
2 cups cooked whole wheat
2 4-ounce cans green chilies
1½ cups grated Cheddar or longhorn cheese
1¼ cups milk
½ cup whole wheat flour
4 eggs
2 dashes Tabasco sauce
¼ teaspoon allspice (optional)
¼ teaspoon cumin (optional)

Brown the ground beef and onion in a small skillet. Add salt. Cover the bottom of a 6 x 10-inch glass baking dish with half of the cooked wheat. Drain the liquid from one can of chilies into Bosch blender. Remove seeds from chilies, and layer chilies over cooked wheat. Spread meat and onions over chilies. Cover with grated cheese. Spread remaining wheat over cheese. Drain liquid from the second can of chilies into blender. Remove seeds and layer over wheat. In blender combine milk, flour, eggs, Tabasco sauce, and spices if desired. Blend well. Slowly pour over casserole. Bake in a 350° F. oven for 45 minutes. Remove from oven, and let sit 10 minutes before cutting. Serves 5 to 6.

Cloud-covered Casserole
Choice of grain

    1 pound ground beef
    1 medium onion, chopped
  ¾ teaspoon salt
  ¼ teaspoon pepper
  ⅔ cup cooked grain
    1 can cut green beans, drained
    1 10¾-ounce can tomato soup
    5 medium potatoes, cooked and mashed
    1 egg
       Milk
  ½ cup grated Cheddar cheese

In a large skillet, fry the ground beef over medium-high heat until lightly brown. Drain off fat. Add chopped onion, salt, pepper, and cooked grain. Saute until onion is tender and beef is cooked. Stir in beans and soup. Transfer to a 2-quart casserole dish. Whip the mashed potatoes with the egg and a small amount of milk until light and fluffy. Drop by mounds over meat. Sprinkle cheese on top. Bake in a 350° F. oven for 25 to 30 minutes. Serves 6.

Kaylene's Vegetarian Lasagna
Wheat

    2 15-ounce cans tomato sauce
    1 medium onion, chopped
    4 ounces mushrooms, sliced
  ½ green pepper, chopped
  ½ cup cracked wheat
    2 bay leaves
  ½ teaspoon oregano
  ½ teaspoon cumin
  ½ teaspoon pepper
    1 teaspoon garlic powder
  ½ pound mozzarella cheese
  ½ pound Cheddar cheese
    8 ounces lasagna noodles
  1½ cups cottage cheese

In a 2-quart saucepan, combine tomato sauce, onion, mushrooms, green pepper, cracked wheat, bay leaves, oregano, cumin, pepper, and garlic powder. Simmer 30 minutes. Shred mozzarella and Cheddar cheeses. In a 9 x 13-inch baking dish, layer one-fourth of the sauce, half of the uncooked noodles, half of the cottage cheese, another fourth of the sauce, and half of the mozzarella and Cheddar cheeses. Repeat layers. Bake in a 350° F. oven for 45 minutes or until lasagna is bubbly and noodles are cooked. Remove from oven, and let stand for 10 minutes before cutting. Serves 8.

NOTE: Noodles may be precooked. Reduce baking time to 30 minutes.

Biscuit Meat Pie
Wheat

    3 cups cubed stew meat
  ⅓ cup whole wheat flour
  ¼ cup cooking oil
  ½ cup chopped onion
    4 cups water
    3 large carrots, peeled and cubed
    1 large potato, peeled and cubed
  ½-1 teaspoon salt
  ¼ teaspoon pepper
    1 recipe Soda Biscuits (page 46)
    1 cup frozen peas

Coat the stew meat with the flour, and brown well in the oil in a large skillet. Add onion, and saute. Stir in water, carrots, potato, salt, and pepper. Cover, and simmer on low heat until vegetables and meat are tender. While the stew is simmering, prepare Soda Biscuits according to instructions. Roll out dough ½-inch thick and large enough to cover the top of a 2-quart casserole dish. Fold the dough in half, and cut a slit in the center. Add the peas to the meat and vegetables, and pour mixture into casserole dish. Place the dough on top, unfold, and press lightly to seal edges. Bake in a 350° F. oven for 30 to 35 minutes or until the biscuit is golden brown. Serves 6.

Saucy Pork
Millet

2 cups uncooked pork roast, thinly sliced
2 tablespoons butter or margarine
1½ cups sliced green pepper
¾ cup sliced onion
¼ cup cornstarch or barley flour
2 cups hot water
2 chicken bouillon cubes
3 tomatoes, sliced
Soy sauce
3-4 cups cooked millet

In a large skillet or wok, saute pork slices in butter or margarine. Add green pepper and onions, and saute until crisp-tender. In a small bowl, combine cornstarch or barley flour with water and bouillon cubes. Add to the skillet, and stir until thickened. Add tomato slices and soy sauce to taste. Heat thoroughly. Serve over cooked millet. Serves 4.

NOTE: Rice or other grains may be substituted for the millet.

Shrimp Creole
Rice

2 tablespoons butter or margarine
½ cup chopped onion
¼ cup chopped celery
¼ cup chopped green pepper
½ teaspoon salt
2 cups cooked tomatoes and juice
1 teaspoon basil
2 4½-ounce cans shrimp, drained
2-3 cups hot cooked rice

Melt butter or margarine in a large saucepan. Saute onion, celery, and green pepper. Add salt, tomatoes, and basil. Simmer for 20 minutes. Add shrimp. Serve over rice. Serves 4.

Note: Cooked millet or barley may be used in place of the rice.

Sukiyaki

This traditional Japanese dish actually arrived in Japan from Portuguese explorers in the sixteenth century.

Rice

1½ pounds sirloin steak
2 tablespoons cooking oil
½ cup chopped onion
1 cup ¼-inch diagonally sliced celery
1 small green pepper, cut in thin strips
1 small red pepper, cut in thin strips
2 cups snipped fresh green beans or 1 16-ounce can cut green beans
½ head Bok Choy, Chinese, or regular cabbage, thinly sliced
1 cup water
½ cup soy sauce
2 teaspoons cornstarch
4-5 cups cooked rice

Partially freeze the steak. Trim off fat, and thinly slice. In a large skillet, saute meat in oil until browned. Remove meat. Saute onion, celery, pepper strips, and green beans until crisp-tender. Add the cabbage and meat to the vegetables. In a small bowl, combine 1 cup water (may be part liquid from the canned beans), soy sauce, and cornstarch. Stir until smooth. Add to the vegetable and meat mixture, stirring well. Cook only 5 minutes or until thickened. Serve over hot rice. Serves 4.

NOTE: Any cooked grain may be substituted for the cooked rice.

Tuna-Rice Curry
Rice

1 small onion, chopped
1 tablespoon oil
1 10½-ounce can cream of chicken soup
¼ teaspoon ginger
2 teaspoons curry powder
1 6½-ounce can tuna
Milk
3 cups hot cooked rice

In a small skillet, saute the onion in oil. Add the chicken soup, ginger, curry powder, and tuna. Stir in milk until the mixture is the consistency of gravy. Serve over hot rice. Serves 4.

Sukiyaki is a zesty combination of crisp vegetables and tender sirloin atop fluffy

Oriental Cashew Chicken
Rice

      4 boneless chicken breasts, skinned
      3 tablespoons soy sauce
    ½ tablespoon seasoning salt
    ⅛ teaspoon onion powder
    ⅛ teaspoon garlic powder
      1 1¼-ounce package tempura batter
        Cooking oil
      3 bunches green onions
      2 cups diagonally sliced celery
      2 large carrots, diagonally sliced
    ½ cup sliced mushrooms
    ½ cup green pepper strips
      1 can water chestnuts, drained
    ½ cup snow peas
    ½ cup cashews
    5-6 cups hot cooked rice
        Sweet and Sour Sauce (below)
        Sesame seeds

Cut chicken breasts into 3-inch pieces. Combine soy sauce, seasoning salt, onion powder, and garlic powder in a shallow bowl. Add chicken, and marinate at least 15 minutes. Prepare tempura batter according to package directions. Heat a small amount of cooking oil to 375° F. in a large skillet or wok. Dip chicken in tempura batter, and fry until golden brown. Keep warm. Remove all but 3 tablespoons oil from skillet. Cut the white portion of the green onions into small pieces. Toss with the celery, carrots, mushrooms, green pepper strips, water chestnuts, and snow peas. Stir-fry in hot oil until crisp-tender, approximately 5 minutes. Add cashews. To serve, pour vegetables over rice in a serving bowl. Place chicken on top, and pour over Sweet and Sour Sauce. Garnish with sesame seeds. Serves 6.

Sweet and Sour Sauce

    ½ cup packed brown sugar
      2 tablespoons cornstarch
    ¼-½ cup cider vinegar
    1½ cups pineapple juice
      2 tablespoons soy sauce
      3 tablespoons catsup
    ⅓ cup diced green pepper
    ⅓ cup crushed pineapple

Combine all ingredients in a small pan. Bring to a boil, reduce heat, and simmer for 8 to 10 minutes.

Dilled Stroganoff
Rice

      1 pound ground beef
      1 cup chopped onion
      1 cup sliced fresh mushrooms
      1 clove garlic, minced
      2 tablespoons snipped parsley
    ½ teaspoon dried dill weed
    ½ teaspoon salt
        Pepper
      1 cup beef broth
    ¼ cup catsup
      1 cup sour cream
      1 tablespoon whole wheat flour
    4-5 cups cooked rice
        Grated Parmesan cheese

In a large skillet, cook beef, onion, mushrooms, and garlic until meat is browned and vegetables are tender. Drain off fat. Stir in parsley, dill weed, salt, a dash of pepper, beef broth, and catsup. Cover, and simmer 10 minutes. Blend together the sour cream and flour; stir into beef mixture. Cook and stir until thickened and bubbly. Serve over hot cooked rice. Sprinkle with Parmesan cheese. Serves 6.

Pepper Steak
Rice

      1 pound round steak
    1½ teaspoons paprika
      1 clove garlic, minced
      2 tablespoons butter or margarine
      1 beef bouillon cube
      1 cup hot water
      1 tablespoon soy sauce
      1 large onion, chopped
      2 green peppers, chopped
      2 fresh tomatoes, chopped, or 2 cups canned
          tomatoes
      3 tablespoons cornstarch
      2 tablespoons water
    4-5 cups cooked rice

Partially freeze the steak, and then slice into paper-thin, bite-size slices. Sprinkle with paprika. In a large skillet, brown the meat and garlic in the butter or margarine. Dissolve the bouillon cube in hot water. Add soy sauce and dissolved bouillon to skillet. Cover, and simmer 10 minutes. Add onion, green pepper, and tomatoes. Simmer 15 minutes. Blend cornstarch and 2 tablespoons water. Add to skillet, and stir until mixture thickens. Serve over rice. Serves 4.

NOTE: Other grains may be substituted for the rice.

Walnut Chicken Teriyaki

Rice

- 2 whole chicken breasts, halved, boned, and skinned
- ½ cup teriyaki sauce
- 4 1-ounce slices mozzarella cheese
- 1½ cups bread crumbs
- 1 cup melted butter or margarine
- ⅓ cup chopped walnuts
- 1 egg, beaten
- ⅓ cup chili sauce
- ¼ cup brown sugar
- 1 teaspoon Worcestershire sauce
- 1½ tablespoons teriyaki sauce
- 3 cups cooked rice

Using a meat mallet, pound chicken to ¼-inch thickness. In a shallow bowl, combine ½ cup teriyaki sauce and chicken. Turn to coat each piece. Remove from teriyaki sauce, and place a slice of cheese on each chicken breast.

In a separate bowl, make the filling by combining ½ cup of the bread crumbs, ½ cup of the butter or margarine, and walnuts. Place about 1½ tablespoons of the filling on each cheese slice. Roll up chicken breasts, tucking in the sides. Roll in remaining bread crumbs, then in beaten egg. Roll in bread crumbs once more.

Place the remaining ½ cup butter or margarine in a frying pan, and heat over medium-low heat. Add chicken rolls, and cook for 10 minutes or until a fork can be inserted in the chicken with ease. Turn often to brown chicken on all sides.

In a small sauce pan, make the sauce by combining the chili sauce, brown sugar, Worcestershire sauce, and 1½ tablespoons teriyaki sauce. Bring to a boil. Place chicken rolls on a bed of hot rice, and pour sauce over chicken. Serves 4.

Chicken-Broccoli Topper

Rice, barley

- 2 tablespoons cooking oil
- 4 cups broccoli flowerets
- 1 egg white
- 1 tablespoon soy sauce
- 1 tablespoon cornstarch or barley flour
- ½ teaspoon ginger
- 1 pound boned, raw chicken, cut into ¼-inch strips
- 4 tablespoons cooking oil
- ¼ cup soy sauce
- ¼ cup pineapple juice
- ½ teaspoon ginger
- 1½ teaspoons cornstarch or barley flour
- 1 cup slivered almonds
- 2-3 cups hot cooked rice
- ¼ cup sliced green onions

Heat the 2 tablespoons cooking oil in a wok or skillet. Add broccoli, and stir-fry for 1 to 2 minutes until crisp-tender. Remove from skillet. In a separate bowl, combine egg white, 1 tablespoon soy sauce, 1 tablespoon cornstarch or barley flour, and ½ teaspoon ginger. Add chicken, and coat thoroughly. In the 4 tablespoons cooking oil, saute chicken for 4 to 5 minutes until the meat is white. Return broccoli to skillet. Prepare sauce by combining ¼ cup soy sauce, pineapple juice, ½ teaspoon ginger, and 1½ teaspoons cornstarch or barley flour. Add sauce and nuts to chicken mixture in skillet; stir until sauce thickens. Serve over rice. Sprinkle with green onions. Serves 4.

Chinese Sundae

Rice, millet

        ¾ cup rice
        ½ cup millet
        3 cups water
        ½ teaspoon salt
        2 10½-ounce cans cream of chicken soup
      2-3 tablespoons milk
        1 5-ounce can chow mein noodles
        2 cups chopped, cooked chicken or pork
        2 tomatoes, chopped
        2 sticks celery, cut into ¼-inch diagonal slices
        ½ pound shredded cheese
      3-4 green onions, chopped
        1 8-ounce package slivered almonds
        1 7-ounce package shredded coconut
        6 maraschino cherries

In a medium saucepan, cook the rice and millet in the water and salt until grains are tender. Drain any remaining water. Pour the soup into a separate saucepan, and dilute with milk. Heat until the soup resembles the consistency of a sauce. On individual plates, build the sundaes, beginning with the rice and millet. Add chow mein noodles, and top with desired portions of chicken or pork, tomatoes, celery, cheese, soup, onions, slivered almonds, coconut, and cherries. Serves 5 to 6.

NOTE: Alternate grains may be used in place of the rice and millet.

Steak Chinese

Rice, rye

        ½ pound round steak
        3 tablespoons oil
        2 cloves garlic, minced
        1 large onion, chopped
        3 cups cauliflowerets
        2 cups thinly sliced carrots
      2-3 broccoli spears, diagonally sliced
        1 small zucchini, diced
        4 cups bean sprouts
        1 cup water
          Soy sauce
      1-2 tablespoons rye flour
        4 tablespoons water
      4-5 cups cooked rice

Cut meat into 1-inch pieces. Heat oil in a large skillet, and saute steak, garlic, and onion. Add cauliflowerets, carrots, broccoli, zucchini, bean sprouts, and 1 cup water. Cover, and steam for 3 to 5 minutes until crisp-tender. Add soy sauce to taste. Mix rye flour and 1 to 2 tablespoons water. Add to mixture, and cook only until thickened. Serve over hot cooked rice. Serves 6.

NOTE: Any cooked grain may be substituted for the rice.

Sweet and Sour Chicken

Rice, rye

        4 tablespoons rye flour
        1 teaspoon salt
        ½ cup packed brown sugar
        2 cups pineapple juice
        ½ cup vinegar
        1 teaspoon minced, dried onion
        2 tablespoons soy sauce
        1 3-pound chicken, cooked, deboned, and
            cut into pieces
      1½ cups green pepper strips
        1 20-ounce can pineapple chunks, drained
        ½ cup slivered almonds
      5-6 cups cooked rice

Combine rye flour, salt, brown sugar, pineapple juice, vinegar, dried onion, and soy sauce in a medium saucepan. Cook until thickened. Add the chicken pieces, green pepper strips, pineapple chunks, and slivered almonds. Return to a boil. Serve over hot rice. Serves 8.

Swiss Steak

Rice, wheat

        4 tablespoons oil
      1½ pounds round steak, trimmed and cubed
        ½ cup whole wheat flour
          Salt and pepper
        1 16-ounce can tomatoes
        ½ green pepper, chopped
        ½ medium onion, sliced
        1 cup water
      4-5 cups cooked rice

Heat the oil in a large skillet. Coat the steak with flour, and fry in oil. Salt and pepper steak. When brown on both sides, drain off excess fat. Blend tomatoes in the Bosch blender. Add tomatoes, green pepper, onion, and water to meat in skillet. Cover, and simmer 1 to 2 hours or until meat is tender. Stir occasionally. Serve over hot rice. Serves 6.

NOTE: Other grains may be used in place of the rice.

Felafel Pockets

Wheat

    1 pound dried garbanzo beans
       Water
    ½ cup cooked cracked wheat
    1 medium onion, minced
  4-5 sprigs fresh parsley, chopped
    1 clove garlic, minced
    1 teaspoon ground cumin
    2 teaspoons coriander (optional)
    ½ teaspoon baking powder
       Salt and pepper
       Deep-fat cooking oil
  6-8 Pita Breads (page 40)
       Alfalfa sprouts
       Chopped tomatoes
       Yogurt or sour cream
       Salsa

Soak beans in water to cover for 2½ hours. Drain water, and grind beans in the Bosch meat mincer or pound into tiny pieces. Add the remaining ingredients, and pound together to form a paste. Let rest 30 minutes. Form into small walnut-size balls, and let rest another 15 minutes. Fry in hot, 375° F. deep-fat cooking oil until golden brown. Place hot in Pita Bread with alfalfa sprouts and chopped tomatoes. Serve with yogurt or sour cream and salsa. Serves 6 to 8.

Barley-stuffed Pita Bread

Barley

     1 pound ground beef
     1 large onion, chopped
     1 cup chopped green pepper
     1 clove garlic, minced
     2 cups cooked tomatoes
     1 tablespoon chili powder
     1 teaspoon cumin
     1 teaspoon oregano
     1 cup barley
  1 ½ cups water
        Salt and pepper
   6-8 Pita Breads (page 40)
        Shredded lettuce
        Yogurt or sour cream
        Shredded cheese

Brown the ground beef, draining excess fat. Add the onion, green pepper, and garlic, and saute. Add the tomatoes, spices, barley, and water. Simmer 35 minutes or until barley is tender. Salt and pepper to taste. Stuff into Pita Bread, adding shredded lettuce, yogurt or sour cream, and cheese. Serves 6 to 8.

Note: The amount of chili powder may be varied according to individual preference.

Overstuffed Rolls

Barley

     3 eggs, hard-boiled and chopped
     1 cup diced, cooked chicken, turkey, or tuna
    ⅓ cup cooked barley
    ½ cup mayonnaise
    ¼ cup minced onion
    ½ cup grated Cheddar cheese
  6-12 dinner rolls or buns, depending on size

Combine the first six ingredients in a small mixing bowl. Cut open the dinner rolls or buns and remove the center portion of bread from both the tops and bottoms. Insert filling, stuffing each quite full. Wrap individually in aluminum foil, and bake in a 350° F. oven for 20 minutes. Serve warm. Serves 6.

Ham and Chicken Crepes
Choice of grain

        ¼ cup butter or margarine
        4 tablespoons whole wheat flour
        2 chicken bouillon cubes
        2 cups water
        2 cups diced ham
        2 cups diced, cooked chicken
        1 cup cooked, cracked grain
        ½ cup half and half or light whipping cream
          Salt and pepper
    20-25 Basic Crepes (page 51)
        3 eggs
      ½-1 cup fine bread crumbs
          Butter or margarine
          Chopped fresh parsley

Melt the ½ cup butter or margarine in a medium
saucepan. Add flour, and cook over medium heat for
1 or 2 minutes, stirring constantly. Dissolve bouillon
cubes in water, and add to the flour and butter. Stir
until thickened. Add meats, cracked wheat, and
cream. Salt and pepper to taste. Place approximately
¼ cup of filling on each crepe, and fold or roll as
desired. Cover, and chill crepes 2 to 3 hours. Beat the
eggs. Dip crepes in egg, and then roll in bread
crumbs. Place in a lightly greased casserole dish. Dot
with butter or margarine. Bake in a 375° F. oven for
20 to 25 minutes. Sprinkle with chopped fresh
parsley before serving. Serves 10 to 12.

Turkey Crepes
Millet

        1 cup cooked turkey
        ½ cup cooked chopped spinach, well drained
        ½ cup cooked millet
        ¼ cup grated Parmesan cheese
        1 tablespoon instant minced onion
        1 10¾-ounce can cream of chicken soup
     8-10 Basic Crepes (page 51)
        ½ cup milk
        ¼ cup slivered almonds

In a mixing bowl combine the turkey, spinach,
millet, cheese, onion, and half of the soup. Fill
crepes with turkey mixture, and roll up. Place crepes
with the folded edge down in a shallow baking
dish. Combine the remaining cream of chicken soup
with the milk, and pour over filled crepes. Sprinkle
with slivered almonds. Bake in a 350° F. oven for 15
to 20 minutes or until heated through. Serves 4.

Shrimp-Buckwheat Crepes
Buckwheat

        ½ cup milk
        2 10¾-ounce cans cream of mushroom soup
        2 cups cooked buckwheat
      1½ cups frozen, fresh, or reconstituted green
          peas
        1 4½-ounce can shrimp, drained
        2 tablespoons chopped fresh parsley or ¾
          tablespoon dried parsley flakes
        ½ teaspoon curry powder (optional)
       12 Basic Crepes (page 51)
          Milk
          Green onions, shrimp, or sliced mushrooms

In a 2-quart saucepan, combine milk, one can of
soup, and cooked buckwheat. Bring to a simmer.
Add peas, shrimp, parsley, and curry powder.
Simmer 5 minutes. Fill crepes, and roll. To prepare
sauce, in a medium saucepan dilute the second can
of mushroom soup with a few tablespoons of milk.
Heat through. Spoon over crepes, and garnish with
minced green onions, shrimp, or sliced mushrooms.
Serves 6.

Fresh Corn Quiche
Corn

    3 medium ears fresh corn, cooked (about 1½ cups cooked corn kernels)
    ½ cup chopped onion
    1 tablespoon butter or margarine
    ½ cup shredded sharp Cheddar cheese
    1 9-inch unbaked pie shell
    6 eggs
    1½ cups half and half or milk
    1 teaspoon seasoned salt
    ½ teaspoon dry mustard
    ⅛ teaspoon pepper
    ⅛ teaspoon ground savory
    Parsley (optional)

Cut kernels from corn cobs. Set aside. In a small skillet over medium heat, cook onion in butter or margarine until tender. Do not brown. Sprinkle onions, reserved corn, and cheese into pie shell. Beat together the remaining ingredients, except parsley. Pour over vegetables and cheese. Bake in a 375° F. oven for 35 to 40 minutes or until a knife inserted in the center comes out clean. Let stand 5 minutes before serving. Garnish with parsley, if desired. Serves 4 to 6.

Quick Turkey Dinner Pie
Choice of grain

    1 9-inch double-crust pie pastry
    2 cups cooked, diced turkey
    1 cup cooked whole grain
    1 10¾-ounce can cream of chicken soup
    1 10-ounce package frozen carrots and peas, thawed
    1 8-ounce can onions, drained and halved
    1 teaspoon salt
    ⅛ teaspoon pepper
    ⅛ teaspoon thyme

Line a 9-inch pie pan with pastry dough. Combine the remaining ingredients in a mixing bowl, and pour into pie pastry. Cover with top crust. Seal and flute edges. Slit the top crust in several places. Bake in a 425° F. oven for 35 to 40 minutes. Serves 6.

Creole Pie
Corn, wheat

    1 pound ground beef
    1 16-ounce can tomatoes
    1 12-ounce can whole kernel corn
    1 large green pepper
    ½ cup chopped onion
    ¼ cup whole wheat flour
    ½ teaspoon chili powder
    ½ teaspoon salt
    ½ teaspoon pepper
    1 9-inch unbaked pie shell

Fry the ground beef in a large skillet until brown. Drain off fat. Drain the tomatoes, reserving ¼ cup liquid. Stir the tomatoes, ¼ cup liquid, and undrained corn into the beef mixture. Slice three or four rings off the green pepper, then chop enough of the remaining pepper to measure ½ cup. Stir the chopped green pepper into the meat mixture. Add the remaining ingredients. Simmer uncovered for 5 minutes or until mixture thickens. Pour into pie shell, and bake in a 400° F. oven for 25 to 30 minutes or until pastry is golden brown. Garnish with reserved green pepper rings. Serves 6.

Pasties

Many nations have their own individual meat pie, but the pasty is especially popular with the Welsh and Cornish people of England. They're excellent served hot with gravy or cold for lunch. When found in a lunchbox, they're fondly referred to as a "letter from 'ome."

Wheat

  1½ **cups all-purpose flour**
  1½ **cups whole wheat flour**
  1½ **teaspoons salt**
  ½ **cup butter or margarine**
  ½ **cup shortening**
  5 **tablespoons water**
    Cooked Filling or Raw Filling (below)
  1 **egg yolk**
  1 **tablespoon water**

Combine the flours, salt, butter or margarine, and shortening in the Bosch bowl. Using the wire whips, mix until flours resemble the texture of cornmeal. Add water, and stir only enough to combine. Chill dough 1 hour. Roll out to ⅛-inch thickness. Cut with a large cutter the size of a tuna can or to the size of a salad plate, depending on the size of pasty desired. Spoon filling onto one side of each dough circle and fold over, pressing edges together. Place on a baking sheet, and brush with the egg yolk mixed with 1 tablespoon water. Bake as the filling recipe directs. Makes 6 to 8 large or 15 small.

Cooked Filling

  ½ **pound ground beef**
  1 **small onion, chopped**
  1 **clove garlic, minced**
  ½ **cup cracked grain**
 1-1½ **cups water**
  1 **small potato, unpeeled and shredded**
  1 **small carrot, unpeeled and shredded**
    Salt and pepper

Lightly brown the ground beef in a large skillet. Drain off excess liquid. Add the onion and garlic, and saute. Add grain, and cook until lightly brown. Add 2 cups of the water, cover skillet, and simmer for 10 minutes. Check moisture content, adding remaining 1 cup water if necessary. Ten minutes before grain is tender, add shredded potato and carrot. Salt and pepper to taste. Mixture should be thick.

Baking: Bake in a 425° F. oven for 10 to 12 minutes or until golden brown.

Raw Filling

  1 **10-ounce flank steak**
  1 **small onion**
  2 **medium potatoes**
  1 **carrot**
    Salt and pepper
    Butter
  2 **tablespoons melted butter**
  ½ **cup water**

Chop meat and vegetables into very small pieces, or use the #8 or #9 cutting disc on the Bosch meat mincer. Mix thoroughly, and salt and pepper to taste. After placing filling on pasty dough, place a dab of butter on top of the vegetable-meat mixture before folding over the pastry.

Baking: Cut a 1-inch slit in the top of each pasty. Bake in a 375° F. oven for 40 minutes. Combine the 2 tablespoons melted butter with the ½ cup water, and divide among the pasties being baked, pouring the butter-water mixture through the slit on top. Bake an additional 10 minutes.

Burger Bundles
Choice of grain

  1 **cup herb stuffing mix**
  1 **pound ground beef**
  ½ **cup cracked cooked grain**
  ⅓ **cup evaporated milk**
  1 **cup cream of mushroom soup**
  2 **teaspoons Worcestershire sauce**
  1 **tablespoon catsup**

Prepare stuffing according to package instructions. Combine beef, cracked grain, and evaporated milk in a small bowl. Mix well. Divide into six equal portions, and shape into flat circles approximately ⅜ inch in diameter. Place stuffing in the center of each circle, and draw beef edges over stuffing. Seal well. Transfer to a lightly greased 9 x 13-inch baking dish. In a small saucepan, combine soup, Worcestershire sauce, and catsup. Heat until bubbly. Pour over meat, and bake uncovered in a 350° F. oven for 45 to 50 minutes. Serves 6.

Pizza
Wheat, rye

        2   cups rye flour
        6   cups whole wheat flour
        2   teaspoons salt
    1 ½   cups milk, warmed
        2   tablespoons yeast
        1   cup butter or margarine, softened
        7   eggs
            Pizza Sauce (below)
            Selected toppings

Combine flours and salt in Bosch bowl. Pour in milk, and sprinkle yeast over milk. Allow yeast to activate. Add butter or margarine and eggs. Knead for 10 to 12 minutes. Cover, and let rise for 45 minutes. Knead to release air pockets. Oil hands and shape dough on a lightly greased pizza pan. Let rise 15 to 20 minutes. Prebake in a 450° to 500° F. oven for 5 minutes. Cover with Pizza Sauce and selected toppings. Bake in a 400° F. oven for 20 to 30 minutes. Makes 4 14-inch pizzas.

Pizza Sauce

        1   onion, finely chopped
        2   cloves garlic, minced
      ¼   cup olive oil
        4   cups tomatoes, peeled and sliced, or
            4 cups chopped canned tomatoes,
                drained
        1   tablespoon basil
            Salt and pepper

Saute onion and garlic in oil. Add tomatoes, and simmer until thick, approximately 1 hour. Stir occasionally. Add basil, and salt and pepper to taste.

Corn Dogs
Corn, wheat

      ½   cup cornmeal
      ½   cup whole wheat flour
        2   teaspoons paprika
        1   teaspoon salt
      ½   teaspoon garlic powder
        1   egg
      ½   cup milk
        2   tablespoons oil
    6-8   wieners
            Deep-fat cooking oil

Measure cornmeal, whole wheat flour, paprika, salt, and garlic powder into a 2-quart bowl. Stir together. In a small bowl, beat together egg, milk, and oil. Add to cornmeal mixture. Combine well. Insert wooden skewers into weiners. Roll each weiner in a little additional whole wheat flour, and then thoroughly coat with corn mixture. Let excess batter drip off. Deep-fat fry for 2 to 3 minutes. Drain on a paper towel. Makes 6 to 8.

Corned Beef Spread
Choice of grain

        1   cup chopped, cooked corned beef
      ½   cup mayonnaise
      ½   cup minced celery
        1   tablespoon minced onion
        2   tablespoons prepared mustard
    1 ½   cups cooked grains

Combine all ingredients, and use as a sandwich spread. Fills 6 to 8 sandwiches.

Tuna-Grain Sandwich Filling
Choice of grain

        1   6½-ounce can tuna
    6½   ounces cooked grains
        2   stalks celery, minced
            Salad dressing or mayonnaise
            Sliced onion, dill pickle, and/or
                alfalfa sprouts

Combine tuna, cooked grain, and celery. Blend in salad dressing or mayonnaise to taste. Add sliced onions, dill pickle, and/or sprouts as desired. Fills 6 to 8 sandwiches.

Side Dishes

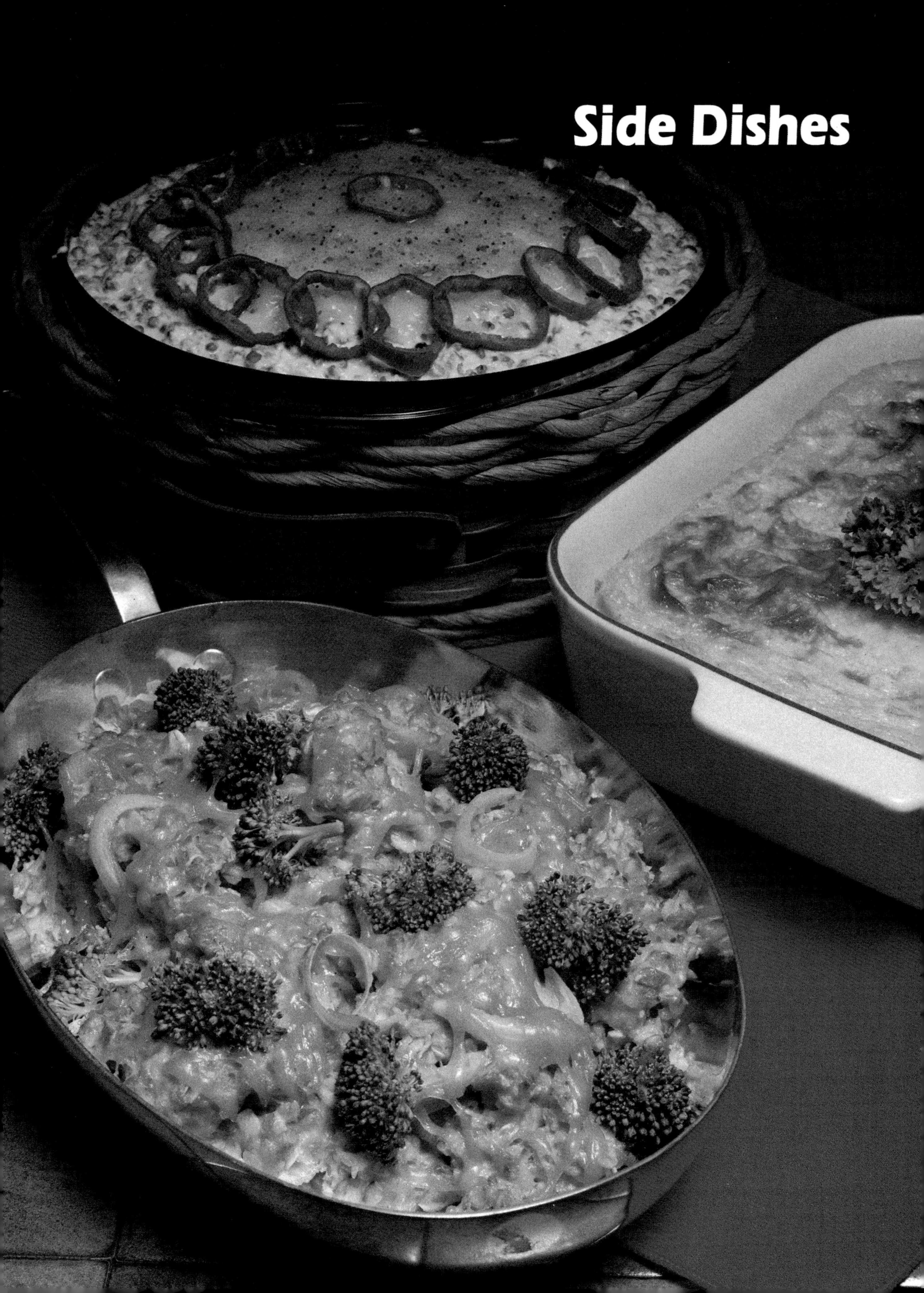

Pine Nut Pilaf

Barley

- ½ cup pine nuts
- 2 tablespoons butter or margarine
- ½ medium onion, chopped
- ⅔ cup barley
- 3 chicken bouillon cubes
- 2½ cups hot water
- ¼ teaspoon saffron
- 3 tablespoons chopped pimiento

In a medium saucepan, saute pine nuts in butter or margarine until lightly roasted. Remove the pine nuts, and set aside. Saute onion until nearly transparent. Add barley, and saute until lightly browned. Dissolve bouillon cubes in hot water. Add saffron. Combine all ingredients in the saucepan, cover, and let simmer for 40 minutes or until tender. Serves 4 to 6.

> Note: Rice, millet or buckwheat may be substituted for the barley.

Barley Bake

Barley

- ½ cup slivered almonds
- 6 tablespoons butter or margarine
- 1 medium onion, chopped
- 1 cup barley
- ½ cup minced fresh parsley
- ¼ teaspoon salt
- ¼ teaspoon pepper
- 2 14-ounce cans beef or chicken broth
- ¼ cup minced fresh chives
  Parsley

In a medium skillet, lightly saute almonds in 2 tablespoons of the butter or margarine. Place in a small bowl, and set aside. Melt the remaining 4 tablespoons butter or margarine in the skillet. Add onion and barley. Stir-fry until barley is lightly browned. Remove from heat. Pour into a 1½-quart casserole dish. Add almonds, minced parsley, salt, pepper, and broth. Bake, uncovered, in a 375° F. oven for 45 minutes or until barley is tender and liquid is absorbed. Sprinkle with chives, and garnish with additional fresh parsley. Serves 6.

Buckwheat Broccoli

Buckwheat

- 6 tablespoons butter or margarine
- ½ cup chopped onion
- 1 20-ounce package chopped frozen broccoli
    or 2½ cups chopped fresh broccoli
- 1 10¾-ounce can cream of chicken soup
- 2 cups shredded cheese
- ¾ cup evaporated milk
- 2 cups cooked buckwheat

Melt butter or margarine in a medium saucepan. Add onion and broccoli, and saute until crisp-tender. Add soup, shredded cheese, evaporated milk, and cooked buckwheat. Cover, and simmer for 30 minutes. Serves 6.

Kasha

> Kasha is a popular dish in Russia, especially in the Caucasus Mountains. It is varied by the addition of meats and vegetables.

Buckwheat

- 1 tablespoon butter or margarine
- 1 egg, beaten
- 1 cup whole buckwheat groats
- 2½ cups water or beef bouillon
- ½ teaspoon salt
- 1 teaspoon ground coriander
- 1 teaspoon ground cumin

Melt butter or margarine in a medium saucepan. In a small bowl, combine egg and buckwheat. Add to butter. Cook over medium heat, stirring constantly, until egg is cooked and buckwheat groats are dry and separated. Add water or bouillon, salt, and spices. Bring to a boil, and then reduce heat to low. Cover and simmer until tender. Serves 4.

> NOTE: Cracked wheat or cracked rye may be substituted for the buckwheat.

Main-dish Kasha

Add 1 cup cubed, cooked meat. A chopped and sauteed onion may be added. Selected additions of almonds, mushrooms, and chopped turnips are also delicious.

Corn and Rice Bake

Corn, rice

        2 cups water
        ½ teaspoon salt
        1 cup rice
     1½ cups chopped celery
        3 tablespoons chopped onion
        ¼ cup butter or margarine
     3½ cups frozen or canned corn
        3 cups grated Cheddar cheese
     1½ cups milk
        1 teaspoon salt
        ⅛ teaspoon paprika

Bring water and salt to a boil in a medium saucepan. Stir in rice, cover, reduce heat to low, and simmer until rice is tender. In a small skillet, saute celery and onion in butter or margarine for about 5 minutes. Add to the cooked rice. Stir in remaining ingredients. Transfer to a lightly buttered 2-quart casserole. Cover, and bake in a 300° F. oven for 1 hour. Serves 6.

AnnaMae Swanson's Cheese Grits

A grand example of good southern cooking.

Corn

        1 cup cold water
        1 teaspoon salt
        1 cup corn grits
        3 cups boiling water
        ¼ cup butter
        1 pound Velveeta cheese
        3 eggs, well-beaten
     1-2 tablespoons Tabasco sauce
        1 tablespoon Lawry's seasoned salt

Combine the cold water, salt, and corn grits in a small bowl. Add grits mixture to boiling water in a medium saucepan. Cook 20 minutes or until tender. When grits are cooked, add butter, cheese, eggs, Tabasco sauce, and seasoned salt. Pour into a greased 1½-quart baking dish. Bake in a 350° F. oven for 40 minutes or until golden brown. Serves 4.

Jalapeno Pepper Cheese Grits

Substitute 4 ounces chopped Jalapeno peppers for the Tabasco sauce and Lawry's seasoned salt.

Herb-Millet Casserole

Millet

        1 cup millet
        2 tablespoons oil
        ½ cup diced carrots
        ½ cup diced celery
        1 teaspoon savory salt
     ½-1 teaspoon herb seasoning
        3 cups water

In a medium saucepan, lightly brown the millet in oil. Add carrots and celery. Stir-fry for 1 minute. Add the salt, herb seasoning, and water. Bring to a boil, cover, and reduce heat to low. Simmer for 30 minutes or until millet is tender. Serves 4.

NOTE: Other grains may be substituted for the millet. If using a different grain, begin with only 2 cups of water and add additional water during cooking, if necessary.

Calico Casserole

Millet

        3 cups water
        1 cup millet
        ½ teaspoon salt
        2 cups grated cheese
        4 tablespoons minced onion
        1 cup minced parsley
        2 teaspoons salt
        3 eggs
        3 cups milk

Combine water, millet, and salt in a medium saucepan. Bring to a boil. Reduce heat to low, cover, and simmer until tender. Drain any excess water. In a small bowl, combine grated cheese, minced onion, parsley, and salt. In the Bosch blender, mix eggs and milk. Stir into cooked millet. Pour into a lightly greased 3-quart casserole. Stir in the cheese and vegetables. Place the uncovered casserole in a 9 x 13-inch pan of hot water. Bake in a 375° F. oven for 30 to 40 minutes or until set. Serves 6.

Note: Rice or other grains may be substituted for the millet.

Milo Casa Blanca

Destined to become a family favorite.

Milo

2½ **cups cooked whole milo**
2 **cups sour cream**
1 **7-ounce can diced green chilies**
½ **pound Monterey Jack cheese, shredded**

Combine cooked milo and sour cream in a 2-quart casserole dish. Add diced chilies and liquid. Stir in half of the shredded cheese. Sprinkle the remaining cheese on top, and bake in a 350° F. oven for 30 minutes or until bubbly. Serves 6.

> **Note:** If milo is not readily available, other grains may be substituted. One grain or a combination of grains works well. Cheese may be varied according to individual taste.

Curried Rice

Rice

1 **medium onion**
1 **tomato, fresh or canned**
1 **tablespoon butter or margarine**
1 **teaspoon salt**
½-1 **tablespoon curry powder**
1 **cup rice**
2¼ **cups water**

Peel and slice the onion. Slice the tomato. Melt butter in a medium saucepan, and saute onion over medium heat. Stir in tomato slices, salt, and curry powder. Add rice and water. Reduce heat to low. Simmer until rice is tender, about 30 minutes. Serves 4.

> **NOTE:** Millet may be substituted for or used in combination with the rice. Add additional water when using millet.

Vegetable-Rice Medley

Rice, corn

¾ **cup chopped onion**
3 **tablespoons butter or margarine**
1½ **cups zucchini, sliced or shredded**
1 **16-ounce can whole kernel corn, drained**
1 **16-ounce can stewed tomatoes**
3 **cups cooked rice**
1½ **teaspoons salt**
½ **teaspoon pepper**
½ **teaspoon coriander**
½ **teaspoon oregano**

In a large skillet or saucepan, saute chopped onion in butter or margarine. Add zucchini, drained corn, stewed tomatoes, cooked rice, and seasonings. Let simmer on low heat for 15 minutes. Serves 8.

Fried Rice

Rice

2 **cups water**
2 **teaspoons granular beef boullion or 1 envelope dehydrated vegetable soup**
¼ **teaspoon ground cumin or minced whole cumin**
1 **cup rice**
½ **cup chopped onion**
½ **cup chopped celery**
1 **clove garlic, minced**
3 **teaspoons oil**
2 **cups diced pork or ham**
½ **teaspoon salt**
¼ **teaspoon chili powder**
¼ **teaspoon mace**
 Soy sauce
 Slivered almonds

In a medium saucepan, combine water, bouillon or vegetable soup, cumin, and rice. Simmer until tender. Cool. In a large skillet, saute onion, celery, and garlic in oil. Stir-fry until crisp-tender. Add prepared grain, pork or ham, salt, chili powder, and mace. Season to taste with soy sauce. Heat slowly, and garnish with slivered almonds. Serves 4.

Slivered almonds add crunch to Fried Ric

Orange Pilaf
Rice

   ½ cup chopped celery
   ¼ cup chopped green onions
   ¼ cup butter or margarine
   1 cup rice
   1 cup orange juice
   1 teaspoon salt
   1 cup water
   1 orange, peeled and chopped
   ¼ cup slivered almonds

In a large saucepan, cook celery and green onions in the butter or margarine over medium-high heat for 4 to 5 minutes. Add the rice, and brown lightly, approximately 5 minutes. Stir in orange juice, salt, and water. Heat to boiling. Reduce heat, cover, and simmer for 25 minutes or until rice is tender and liquid is absorbed. Stir in orange pieces and almonds. Serves 6.

South-of-the-Border-Rice
Rice

   2 tablespoons olive oil
   1 medium onion, chopped
   1 clove garlic, minced
   2 cups brown rice
   2 medium tomatoes, peeled and chopped
   4 cups water
   1 teaspoon salt

In a medium skillet, heat olive oil and add onion and garlic. Saute lightly. Add rice and tomatoes. Cook over medium heat, stirring constantly, for 3 minutes. Add water and salt, bring to a boil, and then reduce heat. Cover, and cook for 20 to 30 minutes until rice is dry and fluffy. Serves 4 to 6.

Parsley and Pepper Rice
Rice

   2 eggs
   ½ cup melted butter or margarine
   ¼ cup chopped green pepper
   ¼ cup chopped fresh parsley
   1 clove garlic, minced
   1 small onion, chopped
   2 cups hot cooked rice
   1½ cups sharp Cheddar cheese
   1 scant cup evaporated milk
      Salt and pepper

In a large mixing bowl, beat together the eggs and butter or margarine. Add the remaining ingredients, seasoning to taste with salt and pepper. Transfer to a lightly greased 2-quart casserole. Bake in a 350° F. oven for 45 minutes or until firm. Serves 6.

Rye-Rice Stuffing
Rye, rice

   ½ cup minced onion
   2 tablespoons butter or margarine
   ¼ cup cracked rye
   ¼ cup rice
   1 beef bouillon cube
   1 cup hot water
   ¼ cup chopped cashews
   ¼ cup raisins
      Minced fresh parsley
      Salt and pepper

In a medium saucepan, saute onion in butter or margarine until tender. Stir in grains, and brown lightly. Dissolve bouillon cube in hot water, and add to the grain mixture. Add cashews and raisins. Pour into a 2-quart casserole, and bake in a 350° F. oven for 20 minutes. Remove from oven, cover tightly, and let stand 15 minutes. Stir in parsley to taste just before serving. Salt and pepper. Serves 4.

   Note: Pine nuts, almonds, water chestnuts, or jicama may be used instead of cashews.

Rye Pilaf

Rye

        1 **ham slice, diced**
        1 **cup chopped onion**
      ⅓ **cup diced green pepper**
      ½ **cup diced celery**
        3 **tablespoons oil**
        1 **cup cracked rye**
        3 **chicken bouillon cubes**
    2½ **cups hot water**
        4 **ounces sliced mushrooms**
      ¼ **teaspoon oregano**
      ¼ **teaspoon cumin**
            Salt and pepper
        1 **cup shredded cheese**
      ¼ **cup chopped parsley**

In a heavy skillet, saute the diced ham, onion, green pepper, and celery in the oil. Add cracked rye, and stir-fry for 2 minutes over medium heat. Dissolve bouillon cubes in hot water, and add to the rye mixture. Add sliced mushrooms, oregano, cumin, and salt and pepper to taste. Pour into a 2-quart casserole dish. Cover, and bake in a 350° F. oven for 30 minutes. Garnish with shredded cheese and parsley. Serves 4.

NOTE: Any grain may be substituted for the rye.

Cracked Wheat Pilaf

Pilaf is an ancient Middle Eastern dish. The ingredients were assembled in a heavy pan, covered, and placed on the dying embers from the previous meal. The grains cooked slowly until supper.

Wheat

        4 **tablespoons butter or margarine**
        1 **small onion, chopped**
        1 **cup cracked wheat**
        3 **chicken bouillon cubes**
    2½ **cups hot water**
      ½ **cup vermicelli pieces (optional)**
      ¾ **teaspoon onion salt**
        3 **tablespoons chopped parsley**
        1 **teaspoon thyme**

Melt the butter or margarine over medium heat in a 2-quart saucepan. Add the onion, and saute lightly. Add cracked wheat, stirring to coat the kernels with butter. Stir until lightly toasted, about 5 minutes. Dissolve bouillon cubes in hot water, and add to the cracked wheat. Add vermicelli pieces, onion salt, chopped parsley, and thyme. Cover, and simmer for 30 minutes or until tender. Serves 4.

NOTE: Any grain may be substituted for the wheat.

Cashew Pilaf

Saute 4 tablespoons chopped cashew nuts and ¾ cup sesame seeds in a small amount of butter or margarine. Add to pilaf mixture. Cover, and simmer as directed.

Almond Pilaf

Add ⅓ cup slivered almonds and 3 to 4 chopped green onions to pilaf mixture. Cover, and simmer as directed.

Vegetable Pilaf

Add 1 cup fresh, frozen, or reconstituted dehydrated green peas to the pilaf mixture. Cover, and simmer as directed.

Cheese Pilaf

Rice, buckwheat, barley, millet

      ¼ **cup butter or margarine**
        2 **medium onions, chopped**
        4 **beef bouillon cubes**
      ¼ **cup rice**
      ¼ **cup buckwheat**
      ¼ **cup barley**
      ¼ **cup millet**
      ½ **pound sharp Cheddar cheese, shredded**
        8 **ounces canned mushrooms and liquid**
        1 **cup slivered almonds**

Melt the butter or margarine in a skillet or medium saucepan. Saute the chopped onions over medium heat. Dissolve the bouillon cubes in hot water, and add to the chopped onions. Stir in remaining ingredients. Pour into 2-quart casserole dish, and cover tightly. Bake in a 325° F. oven for 1 hour or until tender. Add additional water if necessary. Serves 8.

Zucchini Grain Patties
Wheat

    2 cups shredded, unpeeled zucchini
    ½ cup finely cracked wheat
    2 eggs
    ¾ cup shredded Cheddar cheese
    1 small onion, chopped
    ½ teaspoon salt
    ¼ teaspoon thyme
    ¼ teaspoon crushed rosemary leaves
    2 tablespoons oil
      Sour cream or yogurt

Combine the zucchini, cracked wheat, eggs, cheese, onion, salt, thyme, and rosemary in a medium bowl. Mix well. Let sit for 20 minutes. Form mixture into patties. Pour oil into a skillet, and fry patties over medium heat until brown on each side. Garnish with sour cream or yogurt. Serves 3 to 4.

Chinese Noodles
Wheat

    2 large eggs
    ¼ cup water
    ½ teaspoon salt
    2 cups whole wheat flour
      Deep-fat cooking oil

Combine eggs, water, and salt in the Bosch bowl. Using the dough hook, add flour, and knead until smooth. Press through the spaghetti disc on the Bosch pasta attachment. Deep-fat fry in hot oil until lightly browned and crisp. Serve with Chinese dishes or enjoy as a snack. Makes approximately 6 cups.

Egg Noodles

Regular egg noodles may also be prepared from this recipe. Shape as desired. Omit deep-fat frying. Allow to air dry before using (approximately 2 hours), or drop into simmering water or broth as they are made.

Stuffed Paranthas (Chapatis)
Wheat

FILLING (Bhaji):
    ½ inch fresh ginger root or 1 teaspoon
        ground ginger
    ½ cup cooking oil
    2 small onions, minced
    ½ teaspoon black pepper
    ½ teaspoon turmeric powder
    ½ teaspoon red chili pepper
    ½ teaspoon coriander seed powder
    1 pound potatoes, skinned and boiled
    1 lemon, juiced
      Salt
DOUGH (Chapatis):
    2 cups whole wheat flour
    ½ teaspoon salt
  ¼-½ cup water
    2 tablespoons Clarified Butter (below)

Finely chop the fresh ginger root. Heat the oil in a medium skillet. Saute onions with ginger root or ground ginger. Add black pepper, turmeric powder, red chili pepper, and coriander seed powder. With a fork, mash the potatoes, and place in frying pan with the onion mixture. Stir-fry over medium heat for 3 or 4 minutes. Add the lemon juice and salt to taste. Remove from heat, and allow to cool.

To prepare dough, in the Bosch bowl combine flour, salt, and sufficient water to knead the dough. Knead as for bread. When dough is soft to the touch, pour Clarified Butter on palms and work into dough. Place dough in a lightly greased bowl, cover, and set aside for 1 hour.

Form dough into small balls the size of golf balls. On a floured board, roll out each ball to a circle ⅛ inch in thickness. Spread a heaping tablespoon of the filling on a dough round (chapatis), leaving a margin around the edge. Cover with another chapatis, and seal edges (a small amount of water around the edges aids in the sealing). Prepare remaining Paranthas in this manner. Heat a griddle to 375° F. Brush melted butter on both sides of each Parantha, then fry each side 2 to 3 minutes. Serves 4 to 6.

Clarified Butter

Melt a cube of butter. The butterfat will rise to the top and a milky substance will settle in the bottom of the pan. The butterfat is the clarified butter. Knead it into the dough. Use the milky portion to brush on the outside of the Parantha.

Such taste-tempting delights! Clockwise from top: an iced Golden Cake with pineapple topper (page 102), individual Fru Cakes (page 103), Peach Pie (page 99), and Cherry Pie with a lattice top (page 99)

Pies and Cakes

Pies and Cakes

Delicious pies and cakes can be made from variety grain flours. Soft wheat flour is excellent for cakes and pie crusts. It creates a finer textured product than hard wheat flour. However, the use of other grains creates some unique and tasty variations.

Rye and wheat flours are interchangeable in dessert recipes. However, the flavor will differ. Both rye and wheat flours are excellent thickening agents, such as for pie filling, but barley and oat flours are unacceptable as thickeners because they go stringy.

Rolled oats and triticale, rye, wheat, and barley flours are excellent choices for cakes. Rice, millet, buckwheat, corn, and milo flours give a sandy texture and have too strong of a flavor for cakes or pie crusts.

If using only whole wheat flour in a cake, replace 2 tablespoons from each cup of whole wheat flour with barley flour to give the cake lightness. When using a cake recipe not in this book, combine the barley flour with the whole wheat or rye flour when substituting for all-purpose flour.

Here are a few hints to improve the quality of your whole-grain pies and cakes:

When rolling out pastry dough, keep it as circular as possible by gently pushing the edges in with your hands. Always work on a floured surface, and occasionally lift the dough to prevent sticking.

When transferring pastry dough to a pan, lay your rolling pin along one edge of the dough. Gently roll the pastry around the rolling pin. Unroll over the pie pan.

Spread 2 tablespoons of cream or evaporated milk evenly over the top crust of a pie to turn it a golden color as it bakes and improve the texture of the crust.

Cut a piece of waxed paper the size of the bottom of your cake pans. Place it in the pan, and add the batter. After the cake is baked, the waxed paper helps the cake remove from the pan intact.

Sometimes cake recipes call for self-rising whole wheat flour. Make your own by combining 1 cup whole wheat flour, 1½ teaspoons baking powder, and ½ teaspoon salt. This flour can also be used in cookies and pastries.

Hot-water Pie Crust
Rye

- ¼ cup boiling water
- ½ cup shortening
- ¾ cup rye flour
- ¾ cup all-purpose flour
- ½ teaspoon salt
- ½ teaspoon baking powder

In Bosch mixing bowl, pour boiling water over shortening, and mix until creamy. Add dry ingredients, and stir only until mixture forms a ball. Cover and refrigerate 2 to 3 hours. Roll out between two large pieces of lightly floured plastic wrap or on a lightly floured surface. Makes 1 double-crust or 2 single-crust pies.

Ever-ready Pie Crust Mix
Wheat

- 3½ cups all-purpose flour
- 3½ cups whole wheat flour
- 4 teaspoons salt
- 1 pound lard

Measure the flours and salt in the Bosch bowl. Add lard. Using the wire whips, cut in lard until the mixture resembles coarse meal. Store in a covered container in the refrigerator until ready to use. Makes approximately 8 single-crust or 4 double-crust pie pastries.

Pie Crust

Single crust pie	Mix	Ice water
8 inch	1¼ cups	3 tablespoons
9 inch	1½ cups	4 tablespoons
10 inch	1¾ cups	5 tablespoons

To prepare pastry, add the amount of ice water shown in chart, stirring only enough to combine. Gather dough into a ball. Roll out on a lightly floured surface. For a baked pie shell, thoroughly prick bottom and sides with a fork. Bake in a 475° F. oven for 8 to 10 minutes or until lightly brown. For a filled single- or double-crust pie, bake as directed in recipe.

Never-fail Pie Crust
Wheat

- 2 cups whole wheat flour
- 2 cups all-purpose flour
- 1 teaspoon salt
- 2 cups lard
- ½ cup cold water
- 1 tablespoon vinegar
- 1 egg

Combine dry ingredients in Bosch bowl. Using wire whips, cut in lard until mixture is the consistency of cornmeal. Combine cold water, egg, and vinegar in a small bowl. Mix with a fork. Add to flour mixture, and stir only until mixed. Roll out between two large pieces of lightly floured plastic wrap or on a floured surface. Makes 4 single-crust or 2 double-crust pies.

Fruit Pie
Wheat

- 1 cup sugar
- 4 tablespoons whole wheat flour
- 1 teaspoon grated lemon peel
- 4 cups fresh fruit, peeled and sliced
    as necessary*
- 1 9-inch double-crust pie pastry
- 1 tablespoon lemon juice
- 4 tablespoons butter
- 2 tablespoons evaporated milk

Combine the sugar, flour, and lemon peel in a 1-quart mixing bowl. Add fruit, and stir until coated. Turn into unbaked pie pastry. Dribble with lemon juice, and dot with butter. Cover with top crust, and brush dough with evaporated milk to ensure a golden crust. Bake in a 400° F. oven for 20 minutes, and then reduce heat to 350° for an additional 25 to 30 minutes, depending on fruit. Crust should be golden brown and filling bubbly. Makes 1 pie.

*Apples, peaches, apricots, blueberries, or cherries are excellent.

Cherry Pie
Rye

- 3 cups pitted pie cherries and juice
- 1½ cups sugar
- 4 tablespoons rye flour
- 1 tablespoon butter or margarine
- ½ teaspoon red food coloring
- 2 teaspoons almond flavoring
- 1 9-inch double-crust pie pastry
- 2 tablespoons cream or evaporated milk

Drain pie cherries, reserving juice. Measure ¾ cup. Combine sugar and rye flour in a medium saucepan, and mix until no lumps remain. Stir in ¾ cup cherry juice. Cook over medium-high heat until thickened, stirring constantly. Add cherries, butter or margarine, food coloring, and almond flavoring. Pour into pastry-lined pan. Cover with top crust which has been slit to allow steam to escape. Seal and flute edges. Spread cream over top crust. Bake in a 400° F. oven for 55 minutes or until browned and bubbly.

Peach Pie
Rye

- 6 cups sliced peaches, fresh or canned
- ½-1 cup sugar
- ¼ cup rye flour
- 1 teaspoon cinnamon
- 1 9-inch double-crust pie pastry

Mix peaches, sugar, flour, and cinnamon. Pour into a pastry-lined pie pan. Cover with top crust which has been slit to allow steam to escape. Seal and flute edges. Fit a piece of aluminum foil around the edge to prevent excess browning. Remove during the last 15 minutes of baking. Bake in a 425° F. oven for 45 to 50 minutes.

Note: For a flavor variation, omit the cinnamon and add ¼ teaspoon nutmeg and ¼ teaspoon almond flavoring. Sliced apples may be used instead of the peaches.

Lemon Cake Pie
Wheat

        3   eggs, separated
        ⅔   cup lemon juice
        1   cup milk
      1¼   cups sugar
        ⅓   cup whole wheat flour
        1   9-inch unbaked pie shell
            Whipped cream

In a mixing bowl, beat egg yolks until well blended. Add lemon juice and milk. Beat again. Add sugar and whole wheat flour, and whip until smooth. In Bosch bowl, whip egg whites until they peak. Fold lemon mixture into egg whites until blended. Pour into unbaked pie shell. Bake in a 350°F. oven for 45 minutes or until top is golden brown. Cool. Serve with whipped cream.

Pear Pie
Wheat

      5-6   cups sliced fresh pears
        ½   cup sugar
        1   teaspoon grated lemon peel
        3   tablespoons lemon juice
        1   9-inch unbaked pie shell
        ½   cup whole wheat flour
        ½   cup sugar
        ½   teaspoon ginger
        ½   teaspoon cinnamon
        ¼   teaspoon mace
        ⅓   cup butter
            Whipped cream

Combine sliced pears with ½ cup sugar, lemon peel, and lemon juice. Turn into unbaked pie shell. To make the topping, combine the whole wheat flour, sugar, and spices. Cut in butter until crumbly. Sprinkle mixture over pears. Bake in a 400° F. oven for 45 minutes or until pears are tender. Serve warm with sweetened whipped cream.

Banana Cream Pie
Wheat, rye

        2   cups milk
        3   tablespoons whole wheat flour
        2   tablespoons rye flour
        ½   cup sugar
        ¼   teaspoon salt
        3   egg yolks
        1   teaspoon vanilla
        1   tablespoon butter
        2   firm, ripe bananas
        1   9-inch baked pie shell
MERINGUE:
        3   egg whites
        ¼   teaspoon cream of tartar
        6   tablespoons powdered sugar
        ½   teaspoon vanilla

Scald the milk in a medium saucepan. Mix dry ingredients together in a small bowl, and add to the hot milk. Stir until thick and smooth. Beat egg yolks in a separate bowl. To temper eggs, spoon 2 to 3 tablespoons of the hot pudding into the eggs, and stir. Add eggs to the pudding. After mixture thickens, add vanilla and butter. Allow filling to cool. Slice bananas into baked pie shell, and pour filling over top.

To prepare meringue, whip egg whites and cream of tartar until stiff. Add sugar and vanilla. Continue whipping until stiff peaks form. Spoon over pie filling, sealing meringue to the edge of the pie crust. Bake in a 325° F. oven for 10 to 15 minutes or until meringue is golden brown. Chill before serving.

Coconut Cream Pie

Follow instructions for Banana Cream Pie. Omit bananas, and stir ¾ cup coconut into filling before pouring into pie shell. Top meringue with toasted coconut before baking.

Pineapple Cream Pie

Follow instructions for Banana Cream Pie. Omit bananas, and stir 1 cup well-drained, crushed pineapple into filling before pouring into pie shell.

No one can resist Banana Cream Pie, shown here in individual ta

Golden Cake
Wheat, barley

2 cups whole wheat flour
¼ cup barley flour
3½ teaspoons baking powder
1 teaspoon salt
1½ cups brown sugar
½ cup butter or margarine, softened
1 cup milk
1 teaspoon vanilla
2 eggs

Combine dry ingredients in the Bosch bowl. Add butter or margarine and ⅔ cup of the milk. Blend thoroughly. Add the remaining milk, vanilla, and eggs. Beat well. Pour into two lightly floured and greased 8-inch round pans. Bake in a 350° F. oven for 30 to 35 minutes or until cake tests done. Cool 10 minutes; remove from pans. Frost as desired.

Pineapple Upside-down Cake

Pour ¼ cup melted butter or margarine in a 9 x 13-inch pan. Spread 1 cup packed brown sugar evenly over the melted butter. Position pineapple rings on top of brown sugar. Place a maraschino cherry in the center of each ring. Pour Golden Cake batter over all. Bake in a 350° F. oven for 45 minutes. Invert cake, and serve warm with whipped cream.

Strawberry Shortcake

Bake Golden Cake in a 9 x 13-inch pan. Cut into serving pieces. Slice each piece in half horizontally. Spoon sweetened strawberries over the first layer, replace the upper layer, and cover with additional strawberries. Garnish with whipped cream.

Pineapple Topper

Bake Golden Cake in a 9 x 13-inch pan. Combine 1 cup crushed pineapple, drained, ¼ cup butter or margarine, 1 cup packed brown sugar, 1⅓ cups coconut, and ½ cup walnuts. Mix until smooth, and spread on cake. Broil 3 inches from heat for 2 minutes or until bubbly.

Peach Topper

Bake Golden Cake in a 9 x 13-inch pan. Combine ½ cup water, 1 cup sugar, and 1 envelope Knox unflavored gelatin in the top of a double boiler. Stir well, and cook 10 minutes. Slice or mash one No. 2½ can or 1-quart peaches, drained. Combine with gelatin mixture, and chill thoroughly. Spread over cooled cake.

Gingerbread
Wheat, barley

½ cup brown sugar
½ cup butter or margarine, softened
1 egg
1 cup molasses
2⅓ cups whole wheat flour
2 tablespoons barley flour
1 teaspoon cinnamon
1 teaspoon ginger
½ teaspoon cloves
1½ teaspoons baking soda
½ teaspoon salt
1 cup hot water

Cream sugar and butter or margarine in the Bosch mixing bowl. Add egg and molasses. Mix well. In a separate bowl, combine the dry ingredients. Add to the batter, mixing well. Add hot water, and stir until smooth. Pour into a greased and floured 9 x 9-inch pan. Bake in a 350° F. oven for 35 minutes or until cake tests done. Serve warm.

Gingerbread Upside-down Cake

Melt ¼ cup butter or margarine in a 9 x 13-inch pan. Add 1½ cups brown sugar, and distribute evenly in the pan. Arrange pear halves, cut side down, in pan. Pour Gingerbread batter over fruit, and bake as directed. Other fruits can be used, such as sliced apples, pineapple rings, peach halves, or fruit cocktail.

Hurry-up Cake
Wheat, barley

¾ cup brown sugar
¾ cup whole wheat flour
¼ cup barley flour
1½ teaspoons baking powder
¼ teaspoon salt
1 egg
Cooking oil
½ cup milk
Almond or lemon extract (optional)
Nutmeg (optional)

Combine the dry ingredients in Bosch mixing bowl. Break egg into a 1-cup measuring cup, and add enough cooking oil to measure ½ cup. Add milk, and stir with a fork to combine. Combine liquid and dry ingredients, and stir well. Season to taste with almond or lemon flavoring or nutmeg. Pour into a well-greased and floured 9-inch round cake pan. Bake in a 350° F. oven for 30 minutes or until cake tests done. Cool 10 minutes; remove from pan. Cake may be frosted; served with a warm caramel, chocolate, or lemon sauce; or used for strawberry shortcake.

NOTE: Recipe may be doubled to fill a 9 x 13-inch pan.

Oatmeal-Rye Cake

Rye, oats, barley

- ½ **cup butter or margarine, softened**
- 2 **cups brown sugar**
- 2 **eggs**
- 1 **teaspoon vanilla**
- 3 **tablespoons barley flour**
- 1¼ **cups rye flour**
- 1 **teaspoon baking soda**
- ½ **teaspoon salt**
- ¾ **teaspoon cinnamon**
- ¼ **teaspoon nutmeg**
- 1¼ **cups water**
- 1 **cup rolled oats, quick-cooking or old-fashioned**
  Brown Sugar Frosting (below)

Cream together the butter or margarine and brown sugar in the Bosch mixing bowl. Add eggs and vanilla, and mix well. Combine barley and rye flours with the soda, salt, cinnamon, and nutmeg. Alternately add the dry ingredients and water to the creamed mixture. Stir in rolled oats. Batter will be thin. Pour into a greased 9 x 13-inch baking dish. Bake in a 350° F. oven for 30 minutes. Spread Brown Sugar frosting on cake while still warm. Broil until golden brown.

Brown Sugar Frosting

- ¾ **cup brown sugar**
- ⅓ **cup butter or margarine, softened**
- 4½ **tablespoons light cream**
- 1 **cup coconut**

Mix ingredients together until well blended.

Wacky Cake

Wheat, barley

- 2 **cups whole wheat flour**
- ¼ **cup barley flour**
- 1½ **cups brown sugar**
- 4 **tablespoons cocoa or carob powder**
- 1½ **teaspoons baking soda**
- ¾ **teaspoon salt**
- ½ **cup butter or margarine, melted**
- 1½ **teaspoons vinegar**
- 1½ **teaspoons vanilla**
- 1½ **cups cold water**

Mix dry ingredients in a 9 x 13-inch pan. Make three holes in the dry ingredients. Pour butter or margarine in one hole, vinegar in the second, and vanilla in the third. Pour cold water over all, and stir rapidly with a fork until well mixed. Bake in a 350° F. oven for 25 minutes or until cake tests done. Cool in pan. Frost as desired.

Fruit Cake

Wheat

- ⅔ **cup butter or margarine**
- ¼ **cup molasses**
- ⅔ **cup packed brown sugar**
- 2 **eggs**
- 1 **pound candied mixed fruit**
- ½ **teaspoon nutmeg**
- ½ **teaspoon baking soda**
- 1 **teaspoon baking powder**
- 2 **cups whole wheat flour**
- ½ **teaspoon salt**
- 2 **teaspoons cinnamon**
- 1 **cup water or fruit juice**
- 1 **cup raisins**
- ½ **cup pecans**

Combine butter or margarine, molasses, and brown sugar in Bosch mixing bowl. Add eggs and mixed fruit. Combine dry ingredients in a separate bowl. Alternately add the dry ingredients and water or fruit juice to the fruit mixture. Add raisins and pecans. Cut a brown grocery bag to fit a 9 x 5 x 3-inch loaf pan, and grease the paper well. Pour cake batter into lined loaf pan, and bake in a 275° F. oven for 2½ to 3 hours or until a toothpick inserted in the center comes out clean. Cool in pan.

Honey Angel Cake

Rye, barley

1½-2 **teaspoons nutmeg**
  ½ **teaspoon cinnamon**
  1 **cup rye flour**
  ½ **cup barley flour**
 12 **large egg whites, room temperature**
  ½ **teaspoon salt**
 1½ **teaspoons cream of tartar**
  1 **teaspoon vanilla extract**
 1½ **cups honey**

Combine spices and flours, and set aside. Pour egg whites into Bosch bowl, add salt, and whip until frothy. Add cream of tartar, and whip until the egg whites peak. Add vanilla extract. While continuing to whip the whites, gradually drizzle the honey into the batter. Stop the Bosch, and sprinkle half of the flour mixture into the beaten egg whites. Using the pulsing motion, gently mix in the flour. When the flour is only partially blended, sprinkle the remainder of the flour mixture over the batter, and pulse to nearly combine. Remove the bowl from the machine, and with a rubber spatula, gently complete the folding action. Pour into an ungreased tube pan, and bake on the bottom rack in a 275° F. oven for 1 hour. Remove from oven, and invert to cool. Frost or serve with fresh fruit as desired.

Almond Chiffon Cake

Rye, wheat, barley

  1 **cup rye flour**
  1 **cup whole wheat flour**
  ¼ **cup barley flour**
 1½ **cups sugar**
  3 **teaspoons baking powder**
  ¾ **teaspoon salt**
  ½ **cup salad oil**
  ¾ **cup water**
  5 **large egg yolks**
  1 **teaspoon almond flavoring**
  1 **cup egg whites, room temperature**
  ½ **teaspoon cream of tartar**

Combine the dry ingredients in a large bowl. Make a depression in the center, and pour in the oil, water, egg yolks, and almond flavoring. Blend until satiny and light in color. Combine egg whites and cream of tartar in Bosch bowl. Beat until stiff. Add the

whites to the batter, and gently fold in. Pour into an angel food tube pan, and bake on the bottom rack in a preheated 325° F. oven for 1 hour and 10 minutes. Invert to cool. Remove from pan when completely cool. Frost as desired.

Angel Food Cake

Wheat, barley

  1 **cup whole wheat flour**
  ½ **cup barley flour**
  ¾ **cup sugar**
 1¾ **cups egg whites, room temperature**
  ½ **teaspoon salt**
 1½ **teaspoons cream of tartar**
  ¾ **cup sugar**
  1 **teaspoon almond extract**

In a small mixing bowl, stir together whole wheat and barley flours and ¾ cup sugar. Combine egg whites and salt in the Bosch bowl, and whip until frothy. Add cream of tartar. Continue beating until egg whites stand in peaks. Slowly add remaining ¾ cup sugar and almond extract. Whip until glossy. Spoon flour mixture into egg white mixture, 1 tablespoon at a time. Fold gently, leaving some flour not quite mixed in each time. On final addition of flour, gently mix all flour into batter. Pour into an ungreased tube pan, and bake on the bottom rack in a 325° F. oven for 60 minutes. Frost as desired.

NOTE: Two cups of powdered sugar may be used instead of the 1½ cups granulated sugar. Brown sugar may also be used, but the cake will not be as light. Raisins, dried prunes, nuts, or grated orange peel may be added for variety. At high altitudes, if cake pulls away from the sides of the pan, on subsequent bakings, add an additional ¼ cup whole wheat flour.

Chocolate-lovers' Cake
Wheat

    3 cups whole wheat flour
    2 cups sugar
    ½ cup cocoa
    3 teaspoons baking soda
    1 teaspoon baking powder
    1 teaspoon salt
    2 eggs
    2 cups buttermilk
    1 cup cooking oil
    3 teaspoons vanilla
    1 cup hot water
      Chocolate Butter Icing (below)

In the Bosch bowl, combine the flour, sugar, cocoa, baking soda, baking powder, and salt. In a separate bowl, beat eggs, and add buttermilk, cooking oil, and vanilla. Stir together, and then add to the dry ingredients. Beat until smooth. Add the hot water last, and mix well. Pour into a greased and floured 9 x 13-inch baking dish, and bake in a 350° F. oven for 45 to 50 minutes or until a toothpick inserted in the center comes out clean. When completely cool, frost with Chocolate Butter Icing.

Chocolate Butter Icing

    ⅓ cup butter or margarine, softened
    2 ounces unsweetened chocolate, melted
    2 cups powdered sugar
    1½ teaspoons vanilla
    2-3 tablespoons milk

Combine butter or margarine and chocolate. Add powdered sugar and vanilla. Beat in milk until icing is desired consistency.

Hot Fudge Cake
Rye, barley

    1 cup water
    ¼ cup butter or margarine
    ½ cup oil
    3 heaping tablespoons cocoa or carob
      powder
    ¼ cup barley flour
    1¾ cups rye flour
    2 cups packed brown sugar
    1 teaspoon baking soda
    1 teaspoon cinnamon
    ½ cup buttermilk
    2 eggs
    1 teaspoon vanilla
      Fudge Frosting (below)
      Nuts (optional)
      Miniature marshmallows (optional)

Combine water, butter or margarine, oil, and cocoa or carob powder in small saucepan. Bring to a boil. Let cool. In Bosch bowl, combine barley and rye flours. Add brown sugar, baking soda, and cinnamon. Pour cooled cocoa mixture over the dry ingredients. Beat until smooth. Add buttermilk, eggs, and vanilla, and mix thoroughly. Pour into a greased 9 x 13-inch pan, and bake in a 400° F. oven for 35 to 40 minutes or until cake tests done. Spoon hot Fudge Frosting over warm cake. If desired, sprinkle with nuts and/or miniature marshmallows.

Fudge Frosting

    ¼ pound butter or margarine
    3 tablespoons cocoa
    6 tablespoons thin cream or evaporated milk
    1 pound powdered sugar

Combine butter or margarine, cocoa, and cream or evaporated milk in a medium saucepan. Bring to a boil. Remove from heat. Stir in powdered sugar until smooth.

Carrot Cake
Wheat

- 2¼ cups sliced, raw carrots
  Water
- 2 cups brown sugar
- 4 eggs
- 1 cup oil
- ½ teaspoon salt
- 3 teaspoons cinnamon
- 2 teaspoons baking soda
- 2 cups whole wheat flour
  Honey-Cream Cheese Frosting (below)
  Chopped nuts

Cook the carrots until tender in a small amount of water in a medium saucepan. Drain water, and allow to cool. Puree carrots in Bosch blender. In Bosch bowl, beat together brown sugar and eggs. Add oil and cooked carrots. Blend well. Stir in the salt, cinnamon, baking soda, and whole wheat flour. Beat 2 minutes. Pour into a greased and floured 9 x 13-inch pan. Bake in a 350° F. oven for 35 to 40 minutes or until cake tests done. Spread Honey-Cream Cheese Frosting on cooled cake. Sprinkle with chopped nuts.

> NOTE: Cooked pumpkin or squash may be substituted for the cooked carrots. Rye flour may be used in place of the whole wheat flour.

Honey-Cream Cheese Frosting

- ½ cup butter or margarine, softened
- 8 ounces cream cheese, softened
- ½ cup honey
- 2 teaspoons vanilla

Blend together butter or margarine and cream cheese. Add honey and vanilla, and beat until smooth.

Pumpkin Cake
Rye, barley

- 2 cups packed brown sugar
- 4 eggs
- 1 cup cooking oil
- 2 cups pumpkin
- 1¾ cups rye flour
- ¼ cup barley flour
- 2 teaspoons baking soda
- 2½ teaspoons cinnamon
- 1 teaspoon ginger
- 1 teaspoon nutmeg
- 1 teaspoon salt
  Cream Cheese Icing (below)
  Chopped nuts

Cream together brown sugar, eggs, and oil in the Bosch bowl. Alternately add pumpkin and dry ingredients. Blend thoroughly. Pour into a greased and floured 9 x 13-inch baking dish, and bake in a 350° F. oven for 35 minutes or until a toothpick inserted in the center comes out clean. Cool, and frost with Cream Cheese Icing. Sprinkle with chopped nuts.

Cream Cheese Icing

- ½ cup butter or margarine, softened
- 3 ounces cream cheese, softened
- 1 pound powdered sugar
- 2 teaspoons vanilla

Cream together butter or margarine and cream cheese. Add vanilla and powdered sugar, and beat until fluffy.

Banana Cake
Wheat, barley

        1¾ cups whole wheat flour
        ¼ cup barley flour
        1½ cups sugar
        2½ teaspoons baking powder
        ½ teaspoon salt
        ½ cup butter or margarine, softened
        1 teaspoon vanilla
        2 eggs
        1½ cups mashed ripe banana
        ½ cup nuts (optional)
            Banana Icing (below)

Combine whole wheat flour, barley flour, sugar, baking powder, and salt in Bosch mixing bowl. Add butter or margarine, vanilla, eggs, and half of the bananas. Blend thoroughly. Add the remaining bananas and nuts, and mix for 1 minute. Pour into two greased and lightly floured 8-inch round cake pans. Bake in a 350° F. oven for 1 hour or until a toothpick inserted in the center comes out clean. Cool 10 minutes; remove from pans. When completely cool, frost between layers, on the sides, and on top.

Banana Icing

        3-4 cups powdered sugar
        ¼ cup butter or margarine, softened
        1 tablespoon lemon juice
        1 ripe banana

Combine all ingredients in a small bowl. Blend well. Adjust consistency by adding additional powdered sugar or more banana.

Blueberry Buckle
Wheat, barley

        ¾ cup brown sugar
        ¼ cup shortening
        1 egg
        ½ cup milk
        2 cups whole wheat flour
        2 teaspoons baking powder
        ½ teaspoon salt
        2 cups blueberries, well-drained
        ⅓ cup barley flour
        ½ cup packed brown sugar
        ½ teaspoon cinnamon
        2 tablespoons butter or margarine

Combine the ¾ cup brown sugar, shortening, and egg in the Bosch bowl. Mix thoroughly. Blend in milk. Add the whole wheat flour, baking powder, and salt. When blended, carefully fold in blueberries. Pour batter into a greased 9 x 9-inch pan. Combine barley flour, ½ cup brown sugar, and cinnamon in a small bowl. Sprinkle over batter. Dot with butter or margarine. Bake in a 375° F. oven for 45 to 50 minutes.

Blackberry Stack Cake
Rye, wheat, barley

        1 cup whole wheat flour
        1⅓ cups rye flour
        ⅓ cup barley flour
        4 teaspoons baking powder
        ¾ teaspoon salt
        1¼ cups sugar
        ¾ cup shortening
        3 eggs
        1½ teaspoons vanilla
        1 cup milk
FILLING:
        3 cups blackberries and liquid
        ½ cup sugar
        ⅓ cup whole wheat flour
            Whipped cream

Combine dry ingredients in a small bowl. In the Bosch bowl, cream together sugar and shortening. Add eggs, and beat well. Combine vanilla and milk. Alternately add milk and dry ingredients to the creamed mixture. Beat until smooth. Grease and flour five 8-inch or four 9-inch round cake pans. Divide batter evenly among pans. Bake in a 375° F. oven for 20 minutes or until cake tests done. Cool 10 minutes before removing from pans. While cake is cooling, prepare filling by combining blackberries and liquid, sugar, and flour in a medium saucepan. Cook over medium-high heat until thickened. Cool to room temperature. Spread between cake layers, leaving tops and sides plain. Serve with whipped cream.

Glorified Grain

Choice of grains

        2 cups cold cooked grain
        1 cup crushed pineapple, drained
       24 miniature marshmallows
        1 cup chopped apple, unpeeled
       ½ cup sugar
        1 cup whipping cream
           Whipped cream
           Chopped nuts
           Maraschino cherries

Combine the first five ingredients in a 2-quart mixing bowl. Cover, and refrigerate 1 hour. In a separate bowl, whip the 1 cup whipping cream, and fold into grain mixture. To serve, spoon into individual serving dishes, and garnish with a dollop of whipped cream, chopped nuts, and a maraschino cherry. Serves 6.

Rice Elegance

Rice

       ¾ cup brown rice
        4 cups milk
        1 teaspoon salt
       ¾ cup packed brown sugar
       ½ teaspoon almond flavoring
        1 pint whipping cream
       ½ cup slivered almonds
           Nutmeg
           Whipped cream
           Maraschino cherries

Cook the rice, milk, and salt over boiling water in the top of a double boiler for 1½ hours or until rice is tender. Add brown sugar and almond flavoring. Chill thoroughly. Whip the 1 pint whipping cream. Fold whipped cream and slivered almonds into the cooled rice mixture. Ladle into individual serving dishes, and lightly sprinkle each with nutmeg. Serve with a dollop of whipped cream and a maraschino cherry. Serves 6.

> Note: Millet may be used instead of or in combination with the rice. A little additional milk may be needed when using millet.

Barley Chocolate Pudding

Barley

       ½ cup barley
       1½ cups water
        2 tablespoons butter or margarine
        2 ounces semisweet chocolate
        2 tablespoons sugar
        1 tablespoon cornstarch
       ⅓ cup milk
        2 egg yolks
        1 teaspoon vanilla
       ½ cup chopped nuts
        2 egg whites
        4 tablespoons sugar
        1 teaspoon vanilla
        2 tablespoons sugar
        1 cup whipped cream
           Maraschino cherries

Simmer the barley in the water in a covered saucepan for 45 minutes or until all the water is absorbed. Chill. Into another saucepan measure the butter or margarine and chocolate, and melt together over low heat. Stir occasionally. Blend the 2 tablespoons sugar and the cornstarch, and add milk and egg yolks. Beat until the egg yolks are thoroughly mixed. Add to the melted chocolate, turn up heat, and cook and stir until the mixture thickens. Remove from heat. Add barley, 1 teaspoon vanilla, and nuts. Cool to room temperature. Whip egg whites until they peak. Add 4 tablespoons sugar, and whip again until stiff. Fold into the barley mixture, and refrigerate. When ready to serve, add the remaining 1 teaspoon vanilla and 2 tablespoons sugar to the whipped cream. Layer in parfait glasses, beginning with the barley mixture. Top with a dollop of whipped cream and a maraschino cherry.
Serves 6.

Rice and Raisin Pudding
Rice

- 1 cup cooked rice
- ¾ cup raisins
  Water
- 1 13-ounce can evaporated milk
- 2 eggs
- ⅓ cup sugar
- 1 teaspoon vanilla
- 1 teaspoon lemon flavoring
- ½ teaspoon nutmeg

Mix rice and raisins in a 1½-quart baking dish. Add enough water to evaporated milk to make 2 cups. In a separate bowl, beat eggs and add sugar, vanilla, and lemon flavoring. Add evaporated milk and water. Combine with rice and raisins. Sprinkle nutmeg on top. Set baking dish in a pan of hot water, and bake in a 350° F. oven for 50 to 60 minutes. Serve hot or cold. Serves 6.

Note: Cracked wheat or milo may be substituted for the rice.

Baked Indian Pudding
Corn

- 4 cups milk
- ½ cup cornmeal
- ¼ cup sugar
- 3 eggs, slightly beaten
- ½ teaspoon cinnamon
- ½ teaspoon ginger
- ¼ teaspoon nutmeg
- ½ teaspoon salt
- ½ cup molasses
  Ice cream or whipped cream

Scald 3 cups of the milk. Combine the remaining 1 cup milk with the cornmeal. Add to the hot milk, and cook over medium heat until slightly thickened, stirring constantly. Remove from heat. Stir ½ cup of the cornmeal mixture into the beaten eggs, then add eggs, cinnamon, ginger, nutmeg, salt, and molasses to the pudding. Mix thoroughly. Pour into a greased 2-quart casserole. Bake in a 350°F. oven for 1½ hours. Serve hot with ice cream or whipped cream. Serves 6.

Plum Pudding
Wheat

- 4 cups raisins
- 1 cup chopped nuts
- 2½ cups whole wheat flour
- 4 eggs
- 2 cups molasses
- 2 cups buttermilk
- ½ cup fruit juice
- 1½ cups ground suet
- 2½ cups fine whole wheat bread crumbs
- 2 teaspoons soda
- 1 teaspoon cloves
- 1 teaspoon allspice
- 1 teaspoon nutmeg
- 1 teaspoon cinnamon
- 2 teaspoons salt
  Hard Sauce (below)

Combine raisins and nuts with 1 cup of the flour. Set aside. Break eggs into Bosch bowl, and whip thoroughly. Add molasses, buttermilk, and fruit juice. Blend. Add suet and bread crumbs. Combine spices, salt, and remaining flour. Add to the mixture. Stir in raisins and nuts. Divide into two 3-pound greased containers; shortening cans are good. Cover tightly with foil. Place each can in a large kettle of water, allowing the water to come two-thirds of the way up the side of the can. Cover kettle, and keep water simmering over low heat for 3 hours. Serve with Hard Sauce.

Hard Sauce

- ½ cup butter, softened
- 1 cup powdered sugar
- 1 teaspoon vanilla

Beat butter in Bosch bowl until creamy and light in color, about 5 minutes. Gradually beat in powdered sugar. Add vanilla. Refrigerate about 1 hour.

Apple Pudding
Wheat

- 2 cups packed brown sugar
- ½ cup shortening
- 2 cups whole wheat flour
- 2 teaspoons baking soda
- 2 teaspoons cinnamon
- ¾ teaspoon nutmeg
- ½ teaspoon salt
- 4 cups grated apples
- ½ cup chopped nuts

SAUCE:
- 1½ cups brown sugar
- ½ cup butter
- ½ cup light corn syrup
- ½ cup evaporated milk
- 1 teaspoon vanilla

Cream together the brown sugar and shortening in the Bosch bowl. In a separate bowl, combine flour, baking soda, cinnamon, nutmeg, and salt. Add to the creamed mixture. Add apples and nuts. Pour into a greased 9 x 13-inch pan, and bake in a 350° F. oven for 45 minutes.

While pudding is baking, prepare sauce by bringing the brown sugar, butter, corn syrup, and evaporated milk to a boil in a heavy pan. Remove from heat, and add vanilla. Serve warm over warm pudding. Serves 10 to 12.

Apple-Coconut Crisp
Wheat

- 6 tart apples
- ½ cup raisins
- ½ cup packed brown sugar
- ¼ teaspoon cloves
- ½ teaspoon cinnamon
- ½ cup packed brown sugar
- ¾ cup whole wheat flour
- ½ cup butter or margarine
- ¼ cup chopped nuts
- ½ cup flaked coconut

Peel, core, and slice the apples into a greased 2-quart baking dish. Add raisins. Combine the ½ cup brown sugar, cloves, and cinnamon. Add to the apples and raisins, and mix well. Spread mixture evenly in dish. In the Bosch bowl, blend together the remaining ingredients until crumbly. Pour over apples. Bake in a 350° F. oven for 45 minutes or until apples are tender. Serves 6 to 8.

NOTE: Magic Mill Seven-Grain Blend or rye flour may be used instead of the whole wheat flour.

Apple Strudel
Wheat

DOUGH:
- 2 cups whole wheat flour
- 2 cups all-purpose flour
- 1 cup hot water
- ½ cup oil
- ½ teaspoon salt
- 2 egg whites, slightly beaten

FILLING:
- 6 cups peeled, shredded apples
- 1 cup fine bread crumbs
- 1-1½ cups packed brown sugar
- 5-6 tablespoons cinnamon
- 1 cup butter or margarine, melted
- Whipped cream or ice cream

Combine flours in a mixing bowl. In a separate bowl, mix together water, oil, salt, and egg whites. Make a well in the center of the flour mixture, and pour in liquid ingredients. Knead until stiff. Cover bowl with a towel, and place in a 200° F. oven for 30 minutes.

While dough is resting in oven, combine filling ingredients, adjusting brown sugar and cinnamon to taste. Remove dough from oven. Divide in half. Roll each half into a large, paper-thin rectangle. Spread half the filling on each rectangle. Roll up as for a jelly roll. Seal seams and ends. Place on ungreased baking sheets, and bake in a 350° F. oven until brown and juicy, 30 to 40 minutes. Serve warm with whipped cream or ice cream. Serves 9 to 12.

The aroma of baking apples, cinnamon, and brown sugar is only surpassed by the taste of Apple Strudel

Strawberry Cream Puffs

Wheat, barley

PASTRY:
- ¼ teaspoon salt
- 1 tablespoon barley flour
- ⅔ cup whole wheat flour
- ⅔ cup water
- ⅓ cup butter or margarine
- 3 large eggs

FILLING:
- 2 cups heavy whipping cream
- 1 teaspoon vanilla
- 2-3 tablespoons powdered sugar
- 2 cups sliced strawberries
- 2 tablespoons sugar
- Powdered sugar
- Whole strawberries with stems

Combine salt and flours in a small bowl. Bring the water and butter or margarine to a boil in a medium saucepan. Immediately remove from heat, and add all the flour mixture at once. Beat vigorously until the mixture forms a ball and pulls away from the sides of the pan. Allow to cool for 5 to 7 minutes. Add the eggs, one at a time, beating thoroughly after each addition. Beat until dough becomes glossy and smooth. Run baking sheets under cold water, and then shake off excess. Onto dampened baking sheets, pipe dough from a pastry bag or drop by spoonfuls into eight balls. Allow 2 inches between puffs for expansion. Bake in a 400° F. oven for 20 minutes, and then increase temperature to 425° for 15 to 20 minutes. Cream puffs should feel crisp to the touch. Pastry will collapse if underbaked. Remove from baking sheets, and partially cut off tops to allow steam to escape.

While pastry is cooling, prepare filling by whipping the cream and stirring in vanilla and powdered sugar. Combine sliced strawberries and 2 tablespoons sugar. When pastry is completely cool, cut off tops and remove any doughy membranes. Fill cream puffs with the sliced strawberries and whipped cream mixture. Replace pastry top. Sprinkle with additional powdered sugar, and top with whole strawberries. Makes 8.

Chocolate Eclairs

Prepare pastry as for Strawberry Cream Puffs. Shape into 4-inch long fingers. Bake as directed. Prepare whipped cream filling, omitting sugared strawberries. To make chocolate sauce, combine 1 cup sugar, ½ cup light corn syrup, and ¾ cup water

in a heavy saucepan. Bring to a boil. Grate 3 1-ounce squares unsweetened chocolate, and add to boiling syrup. Reduce heat, and simmer 10 to 15 minutes. Cover, and let cool. Fill eclairs with whipped cream mixture, and top with chocolate sauce.

Deep-fried Puffs

Prepare dough as directed for Strawberry Cream Puffs. Heat deep-fat cooking oil to 375° F., and gently drop teaspoonfuls of dough into the oil. Lightly brown both sides. Serve with jam or fruit syrup.

Cheese Puffs

Add 2 tablespoons Parmesan cheese to the Strawberry Cream Puff dough. Deep-fat fry as directed for Deep-fried Puffs. Serve immediately.

Strawberry Delight

Wheat

CRUST:
- 1 cup whole wheat flour
- ½ cup butter or margarine, melted
- ½ cup chopped nuts
- ¼ cup packed brown sugar

FILLING:
- 2 egg whites
- ½-¾ cup sugar
- 1 16-ounce package unsweetened frozen strawberries
- 1 tablespoon vanilla
- 1 tablespoon lemon juice
- 1 cup whipping cream

Combine crust ingredients in a 7 x 11-inch baking dish. Bake in a 400° F. oven for 10 minutes. While crust is cooling, prepare filling by combining the egg whites, sugar, strawberries, vanilla, and lemon juice in the Bosch bowl. Whip for a full 15 minutes. In a separate bowl, whip the cream. Fold into the strawberry mixture. When crust is cool enough to handle, crumble all of the crust and remove one-third of the crumbs from the pan. Lightly pack the remaining crumbs into the bottom of the pan. Pour strawberry filling on top, and sprinkle with reserved crust. Refrigerate. May be made in advance and frozen. Serves 8 to 10.

NOTE: Two cups of fresh, mashed strawberries may be substituted for the frozen berries.

Fruit Fritters
Wheat

1¼ cups whole wheat flour
½ teaspoon salt
2 teaspoons yeast
1 tablespoon oil
1 cup warm water
1 egg white
1-2 tablespoons milk (optional)
   Apples and/or bananas
   Deep-fat cooking oil
   All-purpose flour
   Sugar and/or cinnamon sugar

Combine flour, salt, and yeast in a small bowl. Add oil and water, and stir to combine. Let rise 20 minutes. The mixture should resemble thick cream. When ready to use, whip the egg white until stiff, and fold in gently. Thin with milk if necessary.

Peel and core apples, and slice into ½-inch rings. Peel and slice bananas into four or five diagonal pieces. Heat deep-fat cooking oil to 375° F. Lightly coat fruit with all-purpose flour. Dip in batter, and fry until golden brown. Sprinkle with sugar or a mixture of cinnamon and sugar.

Note: This batter may also be used to coat fish fillets, shrimp, and vegetables. When preparing fish, salt and pepper fillets lightly before dipping in flour and batter. Vegetables typically used for fritters are onion rings, cooked yam chunks, and green peppers.

Peach Cobbler
Rye

3 cups sliced peaches, fresh, canned or frozen
1 cup sugar
1 tablespoon orange juice
¾ teaspoon almond extract
2 teaspoons cinnamon (optional)
1½ cups rye flour
3 tablespoons sugar
1 tablespoon baking powder
⅓ cup butter or margarine
1 egg
¾ cup milk
2 tablespoons sugar
   Light cream

Arrange sliced peaches in a 9 x 13-inch baking dish. Mix 1 cup sugar, orange juice, and almond extract. Sprinkle over peaches. Sprinkle with cinnamon if desired. Thoroughly mix flour, 3 tablespoons sugar, baking powder, and butter or margarine. Add egg to milk, and blend. Stir into flour mixture only until mixed. Spoon dough over the top of the peaches, and spread as evenly as possible. Sprinkle with remaining 2 tablespoons sugar. Bake in a 375° F. oven for 20 minutes. Serve with cream. Serves 10.

NOTE: Any fruit may be substituted for the peaches.

Cheery Cherries
Rye, oats

3½ cups pitted sweet cherries and juice
1 cup sugar
⅓ cup tapioca
1 cup crushed pineapple and juice
1 teaspoon almond flavoring

CRUST:
1 cup oatmeal
1 cup bran flakes
2 cups rye flour
1 cup packed brown sugar
½ cup chopped nuts
1 teaspoon baking soda
¾ cup melted butter or margarine
1 teaspoon almond flavoring

Combine the cherry juice, sugar, and tapioca in a medium saucepan. Bring to a boil over medium-high heat. Add cherries and pineapple, and cook until thickened. Remove from heat. Stir in 1 teaspoon almond flavoring. Combine the crust ingredients in the Bosch bowl. Mix thoroughly. Press half of the crust mixture into a 9 x 13-inch baking dish. Spread cherry mixture over top. Sprinkle remaining crust over cherries, and press down lightly. Bake in a 375°F. oven for 20 minutes. Serves 10 to 12.

Blintzes

Wheat

     1 cup whole wheat flour
    ½ teaspoon salt
     3 eggs
     1 cup milk
       Cheese Blintze Filling (below)
       Butter or margarine
       Sour cream, brown sugar, and/or sliced
          strawberries

Combine flour, salt, eggs, and milk in Bosch blender. Blend until smooth. Pour 2 tablespoons batter into a hot, lightly greased 6-inch frying pan, tilting pan to evenly spread batter. Brown on one side. Stack browned side up. Place ¼ cup Cheese Blintze Filling in the center of each. Fold in both sides, and then fold from top and bottom to form a small envelope. Over medium-high heat, brown Blintzes on both sides in butter or margarine in a skillet. Serve hot with sour cream, brown sugar, and/or sliced strawberries. Makes about 20.

Cheese Blintze Filling

     2 1-pound cartons cream-style cottage
          cheese
     2 egg yolks, beaten
    ¼ cup sugar
    ¼ teaspoon salt
     2 teaspoons grated lemon rind

Pour cottage cheese into a strainer and drain off excess liquid. Combine all ingredients in a mixing bowl. Mix thoroughly.

Cherry Blintzes

Prepare Blintzes as directed. Omit Cheese Blintze Filling. Fill each with 1 to 2 tablespoons canned cherry pie filling. Fold in sides, and roll up. Brown in butter or margarine. Garnish with sour cream or whipped cream before serving.

Jelly Roll

Wheat, barley

    ½ cup plus 2 tablespoons whole wheat flour
     2 tablespoons barley flour
     1 teaspoon baking powder
    ½ teaspoon cinnamon (optional)
    ¼ teaspoon salt
     4 eggs
     1 cup sugar
     1 teaspoon vanilla
    ⅔-¾ cup jelly or jam
       Powdered sugar or icing

Line a 15½ x 10½ x 1-inch jelly roll pan with waxed paper. Grease the paper and the pan sides. Combine the flours, baking powder, cinnamon, and salt. In the Bosch bowl, whip the eggs until thick and lemon-colored. Continue beating, and gradually add sugar and vanilla. Fold in dry ingredients. Pour into the prepared pan, and spread evenly. Bake in a 375° F. oven for 12 to 15 minutes or until cake springs back to the touch. Invert onto a kitchen towel which has been generously sprinkled with powdered sugar. Remove waxed paper, and gently roll up the towel and cake together from the narrow end. Let rest 30 minutes. Unroll cake; remove towel. Beat jelly or jam with a fork to soften. Spread over cake. Roll up, and sprinkle with powdered sugar or frost as desired. Serves 10.

Chocolate Jelly Roll

Add ½ cup cocoa to the dry ingredients. Prepare and bake as directed.

Cookies

Cookies are an ideal way to use variety grains. Their texture and taste often enhance what would otherwise be a rather ordinary cookie. Some grains, such as barley, oat, rye, wheat, and triticale, can be used as the only flour in a cookie recipe. Other grains, such as corn and buckwheat, have strong flavors which must be mellowed by other grains. They are not the best choice for cookies. Millet, milo, and rice tend to make cookies sandy, crumbly, and dry. When using these grains in cookies, use only a small proportion in combination with other grains.

When a variety flour is substituted for wheat flour, it usually requires more flour than what the recipe calls for. Add additional flour a tablespoon or two at a time until the desired consistency is obtained. Variety flours combine well with wheat flour in cookies. Proportions are usually 50 percent whole wheat and 50 percent variety grain flour. A good multigrain mixture for cookies or brownies is 1 part barley, millet, oats, rice, rye or wheat flour and ½ part buckwheat flour.

When making cookies in your Bosch, use the kneading arm. The dough is often too thick for the wire whips and may place an unnecessary strain on the motor. Use the shortening or margarine at room temperature to increase the ease in mixing cookie dough.

Everyone likes cookies straight out of the oven. Cookie dough lends itself beautifully to this type of spur-of-the-moment treat. Make up a large batch of cookie dough, shape it into a long log, wrap and freeze. Just before dinner, take the dough out of the freezer. It will thaw quickly. Cut slices and place on a cookie sheet. Bake and enjoy.

DROP COOKIES

Darlene's Pumpkin Cookies

Wheat

        2 cups packed brown sugar
        2 cups shortening
        2 eggs
        1 16-ounce can pumpkin
        2 teaspoons vanilla
        2 teaspoons cinnamon
        2 teaspoons baking powder
        1 teaspoon baking soda
        1 teaspoon nutmeg
        ½ teaspoon allspice
        4 cups whole wheat flour
        2 cups raisins
        1 cup chopped nuts
           Cream Cheese Frosting (below)

Cream together brown sugar and shortening in the Bosch bowl. Add remaining ingredients in the order listed. Stir together. Drop by teaspoonfuls onto lightly greased baking sheets. Bake in a 375° F. oven for 12 to 15 minutes. Cool on wire racks, and frost with Cream Cheese Frosting. Makes 15 dozen.

Cream Cheese Frosting

        ½ cup butter or margarine, softened
        8 ounces cream cheese, softened
        1 pound powdered sugar
        2 teaspoons vanilla

In a medium bowl, mix together butter or margarine and cream cheese. Add powdered sugar and vanilla. Beat well.

Zucchini Cookies

An eggless cookie!

Wheat

        2 cups packed brown sugar
        1 cup butter or margarine, softened
        2 cups shredded zucchini
        2 teaspoons almond extract
        4 cups whole wheat flour
        2 teaspoons baking soda
        2 teaspoons baking powder

Combine brown sugar and butter or margarine in Bosch bowl. Blend well. Stir in the remaining ingredients. Drop by teaspoonfuls onto greased baking sheets. Bake in a 350° F. oven for 10 minutes. Makes 4 dozen.

Lo Donna's Oat-Chocolate Chip Cookies

Oats, wheat

          1 cup butter or margarine
      1½ cups packed brown sugar
          2 eggs
          1 teaspoon vanilla
      1½ cups whole wheat flour
      2⅓ cups rolled oats
          2 teaspoons baking soda
          1 12-ounce package chocolate chips
      1½ cups chopped nuts

Cream together the butter or margarine and brown sugar in the Bosch bowl. Add eggs and vanilla, and blend. Combine the dry ingredients, and add to the creamed mixture. Mix thoroughly. Stir in chocolate chips and nuts. Using a ⅓-cup measure, shape portions of cookie dough onto a greased baking sheet, 2½ inches from the edge and 6 inches apart. With a fork that has been dipped in water, press each cookie to a ½-inch thickness. Bake in a 350° F. oven for 11 minutes. Cool on baking sheets for 5 minutes before removing. Makes 12.

NOTE: To store cookies, line a baking sheet with paper toweling. Individually wrap each cookie in plastic wrap, and place on the baking sheet. Bake in a 325° F. oven for a few seconds until plastic shrinks.

Butterscotch Chews

Oats

      2⅓ cups packed brown sugar
      1½ cups butter or margarine, softened
          2 tablespoons vinegar
          1 13-ounce can evaporated milk
          4 eggs
          8 cups oat flour
          2 teaspoons baking powder
          2 teaspoons baking soda
          1 pound raisins
          2 cups butterscotch chips
          1 cup chopped nuts
          2 cups shredded coconut

Cream the sugar and butter or margarine in the Bosch bowl. Pour vinegar into evaporated milk. Add to creamed mixture. Add the remaining ingredients in the order listed. Mix well, and drop by tablespoonfuls onto lightly greased baking sheets. Bake in a 375° F. oven for 8 to 10 minutes. Makes 6 dozen.

NOTE: Six cups barley or whole wheat flour may be substituted for the 8 cups oat flour.

Oatmeal Chocolate Chippers

Oats, rye

          2 cups packed brown sugar
          1 cup shortening
          2 eggs
          1 teaspoon vanilla
      1¾ cups rye flour
          1 teaspoon baking soda
          ½ teaspoon salt
          3 cups quick-cooking rolled oats
          1 cup chocolate chips

Cream the brown sugar, shortening, eggs, and vanilla in the Bosch bowl. Add flour, baking soda, and salt. Blend well. Stir in rolled oats and chocolate chips. Drop by spoonfuls onto greased baking sheets. Bake in a 350° F. oven for 8 to 10 minutes. Cool before removing from pan. Makes 5 dozen.

NOTE: Nuts, raisins, carob chips, butterscotch chips, coconut, and/or dried fruit may be substituted for the chocolate chips. Whole wheat flour may be used in place of the rye flour.

Oatmeal Macaroons

Oats, rye

   1 **cup butter or margarine, softened**
   2 **cups packed brown sugar**
   2 **eggs**
   1 **teaspoon vanilla**
1 ¼ **cups rye flour**
   1 **teaspoon baking soda**
   ½ **teaspoon salt**
   1 **teaspoon cinnamon**
   3 **cups rolled oats**
   2 **cups coconut**
   ½ **cup chopped nuts**

Cream together butter or margarine and sugar in the Bosch bowl. Add eggs and vanilla. Stir in the remaining ingredients in the order listed. Drop by teaspoonfuls onto ungreased baking sheets. Bake in a 350° F. oven for 10 minutes. Makes 5 dozen.

Jumbo Energy Cookies

Barley, oats

   ½ **cup nonfat dry powdered milk**
   ¼ **teaspoon baking powder**
   ½ **teaspoon salt**
   ¼ **teaspoon baking soda**
1 ½ **cups barley flour**
   1 **cup quick-cooking rolled oats**
   ½ **cup butter or margarine, softened**
   ½ **cup peanut butter**
   1 **cup honey**
   1 **egg**
   1 **teaspoon vanilla**
   3 **tablespoons water**
   ½ **cup unsalted sunflower seeds**
   1 **cup raisins**
   1 **cup chopped dried apricots**

Combine dry ingredients in a medium bowl, and set aside. Cream butter or margarine and peanut butter in the Bosch bowl. Slowly add honey, and mix well. Add the remaining ingredients, and mix. Dough will be stiff. Place a heaping tablespoon of dough on a greased baking sheet, and spread to a 4-inch circle. Allow room to expand while baking. Bake in a 325° F. oven for 12 to 15 minutes. Makes 1 dozen.

Oatmeal Sesame Cookies

Oats, barley

   1 **cup packed brown sugar**
   ½ **cup oil**
   1 **egg, well beaten**
   2 **tablespoons milk or buttermilk**
   ½ **cup chopped raisins**
   ¾ **cup sesame seeds**
1 ¼ **cups rolled oats**
1 ¼ **cups barley flour**
   ½ **teaspoon baking soda**
   ¼ **teaspoon salt**
   ½ **teaspoon nutmeg**
   1 **teaspoon cinnamon**

Cream together sugar and oil in the Bosch bowl. Add the egg, and mix again. Add milk or buttermilk, raisins, sesame seeds, and oats. Mix well. Stir in remaining dry ingredients. Drop by teaspoonfuls onto lightly greased baking sheets. Flatten with a fork dipped in cold water. Bake in a 375° F. oven for 8 to 10 minutes. Cookies will be crisp. Makes 3 dozen.

Barley-Raisin Cookies

Barley, wheat

   1 **cup water**
   2 **cups seedless raisins**
   1 **cup shortening**
   1 **cup packed brown sugar**
   1 **cup white sugar**
   3 **eggs**
   1 **teaspoon vanilla**
   2 **cups barley flour**
   2 **cups whole wheat flour**
   1 **teaspoon baking soda**
   1 **teaspoon salt**
1 ¼ **teaspoons cinnamon**
   ¼ **teaspoon nutmeg**
   ¼ **teaspoon allspice**
   1 **cup chopped nuts**

In a small saucepan, boil water and raisins 5 minutes. Cool. In Bosch bowl, cream together shortening, sugars, eggs, and vanilla. Add the dry ingredients, nuts, and raisins and water. Drop by teaspoonfuls onto greased baking sheets. Bake in a 400° F. oven for 12 to 15 minutes. Makes 3 dozen.

Bread-crumb Cookies

Wheat

          3 cups fine whole-grain bread crumbs
          1 cup boiling water
          2 cups raisins or other dried fruit
          1 cup shortening
          ½ teaspoon salt
          2 cups packed brown sugar
          2 eggs
       2½ cups whole wheat flour
          2 teaspoons baking soda
          2 teaspoons cinnamon
          1 teaspoon allspice
          ½ cup nuts

Combine bread crumbs, boiling water, and raisins or dried fruit in the Bosch bowl. Add shortening, salt, and brown sugar. Mix thoroughly. Add eggs, and mix again. Stir together the dry ingredients and nuts, and add to the creamed mixture. Drop by teaspoonfuls onto greased baking sheets. Bake in a 350° F. oven for 10 minutes. Remove from baking sheets to cool. Makes 5 dozen.

BAR COOKIES

Big Batch Brownies

Wheat

          8 ounces unsweetened chocolate
       2½ cups butter or margarine, softened
          5 teaspoons vanilla
        10 eggs
          5 cups packed brown sugar
          2 teaspoons salt
          4 cups whole wheat flour
       1½ cups chopped walnuts

Melt the chocolate and butter or margarine in a small saucepan. In the Bosch bowl, thoroughly mix vanilla, eggs, brown sugar, and salt. Add melted chocolate mixture, and mix again. Add flour and nuts. Mix once more. Pour into two 11 x 17-inch lightly greased baking pans. Spread evenly, and bake in a 350° F. oven for 20 to 25 minutes. Do not overbake. Cool, and cut into squares.

Multigrain Brownies

Substitute 1 cup each of barley, millet, rye, and whole wheat flour for the 4 cups whole wheat flour.

Oat Brownies

Replace the 4 cups whole wheat flour with 6 cups oat flour. The texture will be slightly different.

Prize-winning Brownies

Sinfully delicious!

Rye

          ⅔ cup butter or margarine
          ¾ cup cocoa
          2 cups brown sugar
          4 eggs
       1½ cups rye flour
          1 teaspoon salt
          1 teaspoon baking powder
          1 cup chopped nuts
          1 7-ounce jar marshmallow cream
            Cocoa Frosting (below)

Melt the butter or margarine in a large saucepan. Stir in cocoa. Add brown sugar and eggs. Beat well. Add dry ingredients and nuts, and mix again. Pour into a greased 9 x 13-inch pan. Bake in a 350° F. oven for 25 to 30 minutes. Cool. Spread with marshmallow cream, and then cover with Cocoa Frosting. Cut into squares.

Cocoa Frosting

          1 cup brown sugar
          ½ cup cocoa
          ⅓ cup water
          ⅓ cup butter or margarine, softened
            Powdered sugar

Combine brown sugar, cocoa, water, and butter or margarine in a medium saucepan. Bring to a boil. Remove from heat, and stir in powdered sugar until frosting reaches spreading consistency.

Brownie Mix

Wheat, oats, rye

      2 cups whole wheat flour
      1 cup oat flour
      1 cup rye flour
      4 teaspoons baking powder
      4 teaspoons salt
      8 cups packed brown sugar
   2½ cups cocoa
      2 cups shortening

Combine flours, baking powder, salt, brown sugar, and cocoa in the Bosch bowl. Blend well using wire whips. Add shortening, and mix thoroughly. Store in a covered container in a cool place. Makes 8 batches.

> NOTE: The recipe may be made with all whole wheat flour. Barley flour may be substituted for the oat and rye flours.

Brownies

      2 eggs
      1 teaspoon vanilla
      2 cups Brownie Mix
      ⅔ cup chopped nuts

Combine eggs, vanilla, and Brownie Mix in the Bosch bowl. Blend well. Add nuts. Pour into a greased 8 x 8-inch pan. Bake in a 350° F. oven for 20 to 25 minutes or until brownies pull away from the sides of the pan. Cool before cutting into squares.

Lemon Squares

Wheat, barley

      1 cup whole wheat flour
      1 cup barley flour
      1 cup butter or margarine, softened
      ½ cup powdered sugar
      4 eggs
      2 cups sugar
      1 teaspoon baking powder
      ½ teaspoon salt
      ⅓ cup lemon juice
      1 teaspoon lemon peel (optional)

In a small mixing bowl, combine flours, butter or margarine, and powdered sugar. Press into a 9 x 13-inch pan. Bake in a 350° F. oven for 20 minutes or until slightly browned around the edges. Remove from oven. In Bosch bowl, beat together eggs, sugar, baking powder, salt, lemon juice, and lemon peel, if desired. Pour over crust, and bake an additional 20 to 25 minutes. The second baking will be browner than the first. Cool, and cut into squares.

Pretty Little Pinks

Wheat

DOUGH:
      ¾ cup butter or margarine, softened
      ⅓ cup packed brown sugar
   1½ cups whole wheat flour

FILLING:
      2 envelopes unflavored gelatin
      ½ cup cold water
      2 cups sugar
      ½ cup maraschino cherry juice
      1 teaspoon almond extract
      ½ cup maraschino cherry pieces
      ½ cup slivered almonds

Cream together butter or margarine and brown sugar in the Bosch bowl. Add whole wheat flour, and mix well. Mixture should be soft. Press into a 7 x 11-inch baking dish. Bake in a 325° F. oven for 30 minutes.

While crust is baking, make the filling by sprinkling gelatin over cold water in a small bowl. Set aside. In a saucepan, combine sugar and maraschino cherry juice. Boil 2 minutes. Remove from heat. Add softened gelatin and almond extract. Pour into Bosch bowl, and whip until mixture is stiff. Add cherries and nuts. Pour over cooled crust. Refrigerate at least 2 hours. Cut into squares.

Blarney Stones
Wheat

BATTER:
- 5 egg yolks
- 2 cups packed brown sugar
- 1 teaspoon vanilla
- 3 cups whole wheat flour
- ½ teaspoon salt
- 3 teaspoons baking powder
- 1 cup boiling water

COATING:
- 1 pound salted peanuts
- 2 egg whites
- 1 pound powdered sugar
- 1 cup butter or margarine, softened
- 1 teaspoon vanilla

In the Bosch bowl, whip egg yolks until thick and lemon colored. Add brown sugar and vanilla. In a separate bowl, combine flour, salt, and baking powder. To the egg mixture, alternately add the water and the flour mixture. Beat well. Pour into a greased and floured 11 x 17-inch baking pan. Bake in a 350° F. oven for 30 minutes. Cool. Cut into 40 squares.

To prepare coating, grind salted peanuts in Bosch meat grinder. Set aside. In a small bowl, whip the egg whites until stiff. In Bosch bowl, combine powdered sugar, butter or margarine, and vanilla. Beat in egg whites. Frost the sides of each square, and roll in chopped peanuts. Frost the tops and dip in peanuts; repeat for the bottoms. Frost sparingly.

> NOTE: Chopped pecans, almonds, walnuts, cashews, or shredded coconut may be substituted for the salted peanuts.

Oatmeal Date Bars
Oats, wheat

- 3 cups chopped dates
- 1½ cups water
- 1 cup packed brown sugar
- 1 cup shortening
- 1 egg
- 1 teaspoon vanilla
- 2 cups whole wheat flour
- 1 teaspoon salt
- 1 teaspoon baking soda
- 2 cups quick-cooking rolled oats

Combine the chopped dates and water in a medium saucepan. Simmer 5 to 10 minutes, stirring constantly. Cool. To prepare the dough, cream together the brown sugar, shortening, egg, and vanilla in the Bosch bowl. Combine the whole wheat flour, salt, baking soda, and rolled oats in a separate bowl, and gradually add to the creamed ingredients. Mix well. Divide dough in half. Press half the dough into a 9 x 13-inch baking dish. Spread the cooled dates over the dough. Sprinkle the remaining dough evenly on top, pressing down lightly. Bake in a 375° F. oven for 25 to 30 minutes or until lightly browned. While warm, cut into bars and remove from pan.

> NOTE: Raisins, chopped dried apricots, or other dried fruits may be used in place of the chopped dates. Fruit may be sweetened with honey, if needed.

Granola Bars
Wheat, oats

- 3 cups packed brown sugar
- 2 cups oil
- 4 eggs
- 2 teaspoons vanilla
- 2 teaspoons baking soda
- 1½ teaspoons salt
- 4 cups rolled oats
- 1 cup chopped walnuts
- 1 cup shredded coconut (optional)
- 4 cups whole wheat flour

In the Bosch mixing bowl, cream together sugar and oil. Add eggs, and beat in each additional ingredient as listed. Divide batter equally between two greased 11 x 17-inch baking pans, and spread evenly. Bake in a 375° F. oven for 15 minutes. Cut into squares while warm. Remove from pan to cool.

Date Bars

Wheat

FILLING:
- 1 cup chopped dates
- 1 cup packed brown sugar
- 2 tablespoons whole wheat flour
- 1 teaspoon vanilla
- 1 cup water
- 2 tablespoons butter or margarine
- ½ cup walnuts

DOUGH:
- 1 cup butter or margarine, softened
- 2 cups packed brown sugar
- 3 eggs
- ¼ cup water
- 1 teaspoon vanilla
- 1 teaspoon baking soda
- ¼ teaspoon salt
- 4 cups whole wheat flour

Combine filling ingredients in a small saucepan. Cook until thickened, stirring often. To make dough, in the Bosch bowl cream together butter or margarine, brown sugar, and eggs. Add remaining ingredients, and mix well. Divide dough in half. Roll half into a 9 x 13-inch rectangle, and press into a 9 x 13-inch baking dish. Cover with filling.
Roll out the second half of the dough to a 9 x 13-inch rectangle. Place on top of the filling. Press down lightly. Bake in a 375° F. oven for 30 to 35 minutes. Cool, and cut into bars.

> NOTE: Other dried fruits, such as prunes, raisins, or apricots may be substituted for or used in combination with the dates. Equal portions of wheat, rye, barley, and oat groats may be milled together in the Magic Mill III Plus™ and 4 cups of this flour used in place of the whole wheat flour.

Caramel Nuggets

Wheat

- 1 cup butter or margarine, softened
- 2 teaspoons vanilla
- 1 cup packed brown sugar
- 1 cup chopped dried fruit or raisins
- 1 cup chopped nuts
- ¾ teaspoon salt
- 2 cups whole wheat flour
- Burnt Butter Frosting (below)

In the Bosch mixing bowl, combine butter or margarine, vanilla, and brown sugar. Add the remaining ingredients, and mix thoroughly. Spread in a greased 9 x 13-inch baking dish. Bake in a 350° F. oven for 20 to 25 minutes. Spread Burnt Butter Frosting on warm bars, and cut into squares when cool.

Burnt Butter Frosting

- ⅓ cup butter (no substitutes)
- 2 cups powdered sugar
- 2-3 tablespoons milk
- 1 teaspoon vanilla

Melt butter in a medium saucepan, and cook over medium heat until browned. Remove from heat. Add the remaining ingredients, adding additional milk if necessary.

Adele's Chewy Chip Bars

Wheat

- 2½ cups packed brown sugar
- 2 eggs
- ¾ cup oil
- 1 teaspoon vanilla
- ½ cup chopped walnuts
- 2 cups whole wheat flour
- ½ teaspoon salt
- ½ teaspoon baking powder
- 1 cup chocolate, carob, or butterscotch chips

In the Bosch mixing bowl, combine brown sugar, eggs, oil, vanilla, and walnuts. In a medium bowl, mix together flour, salt, and baking powder. Add to the creamed mixture. Pour mixture into a greased 9 x 13-inch pan, and spread evenly. Sprinkle chips on top. Bake in a 350° F. oven for 25 minutes. Cut into squares while still hot.

REFRIGERATOR COOKIES

Raisin Yeast Cookies

Wheat

> 1 tablespoon yeast
> ¼ cup warm water
> 3 cups whole wheat flour
> ¾ teaspoon salt
> 1 cup butter or margarine, softened
> ⅔ cup sour cream
> 2 egg yolks
> 1 teaspoon almond extract
>   Raisin Filling (below)
>   Powdered sugar (optional)

In a small bowl, soften yeast in water. Combine flour, salt, and butter or margarine in Bosch bowl. Blend until mixture has the appearance of cornmeal. Add the yeast mixture, sour cream, egg yolks, and almond extract. Blend until flour is moistened. Remove from bowl, shape into a ball, and cover and refrigerate 2 to 3 hours. Divide chilled dough into four portions. Roll each portion into a large rectangle ⅛-inch in thickness. Spread filling on dough and roll up, starting at long side. Slice into 2-inch pieces. Place on greased baking sheets with cut side down. Bake in a 375° F. oven for 10 minutes. Roll in powdered sugar, if desired. Makes 4 dozen.

Raisin Filling

> 2 cups raisins
>   Water
>   Applesauce
> ½ cup chopped nuts

Soak raisins in water to cover for 10 minutes. Drain water, and grind raisins in meat mincer. Add enough applesauce to moisten. Stir in chopped nuts.

Date Yeast Cookies

Cook 2 cups chopped dates in 1 cup water until thick. Add ½ cup chopped nuts. Use in place of Raisin Filling. Prepare cookies as directed.

Date Cups

Wheat

PASTRY:

> 1 cup butter or margarine, softened
> 6 ounces cream cheese, room temperature
> 2 cups whole wheat flour
> ¼ cup finely chopped pecans or slivered almonds

FILLING:

> 2 cups chopped dates
> 1 cup water
> 2 tablespoons butter or margarine
> 4 eggs, beaten
> 1 tablespoon vanilla
> 1 cup pecan pieces or slivered almonds

Cream together 1 cup butter or margarine and cream cheese in the Bosch bowl. Add whole wheat flour, and blend. Chill at least 1 hour.

To make filling, cook chopped dates and water in a small saucepan until the water is absorbed and the mixture is thick. Add 2 tablespoons butter or margarine, and cool slightly. Stir in beaten eggs, vanilla, and 1 cup nuts. Set aside.

Form chilled dough into 48 balls and press into small greased muffin tins to form a pastry shell. Spoon in a generous teaspoon of filling. Sprinkle with remaining ¼ cup chopped nuts. Bake in a 350° F. oven for 12 to 15 minutes. Remove from pans to cool. Makes 4 dozen.

> NOTE: One-half cup oat or barley flour may be substituted for ½ cup whole wheat flour.

Caramel Cups

Combine 2 tablespoons melted butter, 1½ cups packed brown sugar, 1 tablespoon vanilla, and 2 eggs in a medium saucepan. Cook until thickened, and then fill cups and bake as directed above.

Jam Balls

Form chilled dough balls, and place in greased muffin tins. Make an indentation in the center of each ball, and fill with a teaspoonful of jam. Bake as directed above.

Sunflower Seed Cookies
Barley, oats

1 cup butter or margarine, softened
2 cups packed brown sugar
2 eggs
1 teaspoon almond extract
2 cups barley flour
1 teaspoon soda
3 cups quick-cooking rolled oats
1 cup sunflower seeds

Combine butter or margarine and brown sugar in Bosch bowl. Mix thoroughly. Add remaining ingredients in the order listed, mixing well after each addition. Roll the dough into logs 2 inches in diameter. Wrap in plastic wrap or waxed paper, and chill until firm. Slice dough ½ inch thick, and arrange on ungreased baking sheets. Allow 1 inch between cookies. Press lightly with a fork. Bake in a 350° F. oven for 10 minutes. Remove from baking sheet, cool on wire racks, and store in an airtight container. Makes 6 dozen.

SHAPED COOKIES

Peanut-Coconut Balls
Oats, wheat

⅔ cup chopped peanuts
⅔ cup peanut butter
1½ cups quick-cooking rolled oats
½ cup shredded coconut
1½ cups packed brown sugar
¾ cup whole wheat flour
½ cup butter or margarine
½ cup milk
1 teaspoon vanilla
  Shredded coconut and/or finely chopped peanuts

Combine peanuts, peanut butter, rolled oats, and coconut. Set aside. In a large saucepan, combine brown sugar, whole wheat flour, butter or margarine, and milk. Bring to a boil. Boil 3 minutes, stirring constantly. Remove from heat, and stir in peanut butter mixture and vanilla. Form into balls, using tablespoon-size portions of dough. Roll in coconut and/or chopped peanuts. Allow to dry. Makes 5 dozen.

Gingersnaps

An old-fashioned favorite to be enjoyed with an ice-cold glass of milk.

Wheat

2 cups packed brown sugar
1 cup shortening
1 egg
1 cup unsulphured molasses
4 cups whole wheat flour
2 teaspoons baking soda
2 teaspoons ginger
½ teaspoon salt
1 teaspoon lemon extract
1 teaspoon vanilla extract
  Sugar (optional)

Cream together brown sugar and shortening in Bosch bowl. Add egg and molasses. Mix well. Stir in flour, baking soda, ginger, salt, and lemon and vanilla extracts. Chill dough thoroughly. Roll into balls using tablespoon-size portions, and space 2 inches apart on lightly greased baking sheets. Bake in a 350° F. oven for 12 minutes or until the top of the cookies crack. Remove from oven. Sprinkle with sugar, if desired. Removed from baking sheets to cool. Makes 4 dozen.

Peanut Butter Cookies
Wheat

2 cups packed brown sugar
1 cup margarine or shortening, softened
2 eggs
1 cup peanut butter
1 teaspoon vanilla
2 teaspoons baking soda
⅓ teaspoon salt
3 cups whole wheat flour

Cream together brown sugar and margarine or shortening in the Bosch bowl. Add eggs. Cream again. Add peanut butter, vanilla, baking soda, and salt, and mix well. Stir in flour. Roll into teaspoon-size balls, and place on lightly oiled baking sheets. Press flat with a fork. Bake in a 375° F. oven for 12 minutes. Makes 5 dozen.

NOTE: One and one-half cups rice, barley, oat, or rye flour may be substituted for half of the whole wheat flour.

ROLLED COOKIES

Sue's High-protein Cookies

Wheat

1 **cup butter or margarine, softened**
1 **cup cream cheese**
1 **cup sugar**
¾ **cup protein powder, any flavor**
2½ **cups whole wheat flour**
2 **cups finely chopped nuts**

Cream butter or margarine, cream cheese, and sugar in Bosch bowl. Add protein powder, flour, and nuts. Mix well. Roll to ¼-inch thickness. Cut with a biscuit cutter. Place on baking sheets, and bake in a 350° F. for 10 to 12 minutes. Makes 3 dozen.

Shortnin' Bread

Mammy's li'l baby loves shortnin' bread.

Wheat

½ **cup butter or margarine, softened**
½ **cup packed brown sugar**
1½ **cups whole wheat flour**

Cream together the butter or margarine and brown sugar in the Bosch mixing bowl. Add the whole wheat flour, and mix well. Roll out dough to ½-inch thickness, and cut with a biscuit cutter. Place circles 1 inch apart on lightly greased baking sheets. Bake in a 350° F. oven for 20 minutes. Makes 12 to 14 cookies.

Scotch Shortbread

Barley, wheat

1 **cup butter or margarine, softened**
1 **cup sugar**
1½ **cups whole wheat flour**
1½ **cups barley flour**

Combine all ingredients in the Bosch bowl. Turn out onto a floured board. If necessary, knead in additional flour until the dough cracks and does not stick to the surface. Roll to ¼-inch thickness. Cut

with a cookie cutter, or cut into 1½-inch squares with a knife. Bake on ungreased baking sheets in a 275° F. oven for 50 minutes or until lightly browned. Makes approximately 2 dozen.

Teething Cookies

Wheat

2 **tablespoons oil**
2 **tablespoons honey**
2 **tablespoons molasses**
1 **egg yolk**
1 **tablespoon soy flour**
1 **cup whole wheat flour**
1-2 **tablespoons milk (optional)**

Blend oil, honey, molasses, and egg yolk in a small bowl. Stir in flours. If dough is dry, add 1 to 2 tablespoons milk. Roll out to ¼-inch thickness. Cut into 1 x 2-inch pieces. Arrange on ungreased baking sheets. Bake in a 350° F. oven for 15 to 20 minutes. Makes 4 dozen.

Index

More Famous Magic Mill Products for Making Magic in Your Own Kitchen!

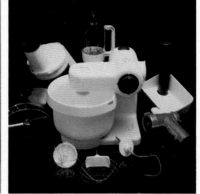

The Magic of Wheat Cookery
The cookbook that unlocks the secrets of successful cooking with wheat. Hundreds of recipes are included: main courses, breads, meat extenders, light and fluffy desserts—all made from 100% whole wheat grain.

The Bosch Compact
The Bosch Compact gives you the advantages of owning four machines in one. It's a mixer, blender, breadmaker and slicer/shredder—all in one small, but powerful—package.

The Bosch Compact mixes, stirs, whips, blends, purees, slices, shreds, kneads, grates and more. Much more.

And its two year limited warranty reflects Bosch's pride in manufacturing excellence. That's why the Bosch Compact is the #1 compact kitchen machine in the world!

Simply Gourmet
A "must" companion to your Bosch Kitchen Machine. 192 pages of recipes specifically written to be prepared with the Bosch and all of its exciting attachments. Elegant and delicious main dishes, soups, salads, pasta, vegetables, desserts and more.

Clip and Mail This Coupon for More Information!

© 1984 Magic Mill   Printed in USA

Become a Magic Mill Family Member

Interested in an exciting, enjoyable and rewarding opportunity? If you are, become a Magic Mill dealer and join our happy family.

Over 10,000 Magic Mill dealers in the U.S. and Canada have found that representing Magic Mill and Bosch products is not only fun but an excellent way to provide a supplementary income.

Consider the advantages:

Excellent Products: Thousands of customers know Magic Mill and Bosch products are simply the best available. Magic Mill stands 100% behind its products—always has, always will.

Dealer Support: You will receive support and training from Magic Mill headquarters, distributors and fellow dealers.

Promotion: If you choose, you may take the opportunity to advance and become a manager, pilot distributor, master distributor—or even the special Associate Distributor opportunity! With advancement come increased earnings, involvement in contests, personal recognition, and more.

Be Your Own Boss: Being a member of our family gives you the opportunity to go into business for yourself. You set your hours, your appointments, your personal advancement schedule.

For further information, please contact your Magic Mill distributor or dealer—or Magic Mill at (801) 322-1668. We will be happy to refer you to your nearest distributor.

The Associate Distributor Opportunity

Few business opportunities allow a person to significantly affect other people's lives, as well as realize an excellent income.

One such opportunity is Magic Mill's Associate Distributor program.

Through it, you will meet new people, improve their lives by sharing the benefits of proper nutrition and better health, help them save time and money, and earn a satisfying income.

As a Magic Mill Associate Distributor, you represent the world's finest kitchen appliances. You own your own business. You work for yourself.

Magic Mill will stand 100% beside you in this endeavor. We will provide unparalleled training and sales support to help make your dream come true.

Magic Mill's Associate Distributor program is an opportunity to strike out on your own. Do so today.

Opportunities are available in various areas of the United States and Canada. Ask your Magic Mill distributor for further information, or call (801) 322-1668.